Keeping the Sal

By

BEN R. VARDAMAN

EDUCATIONAL DIRECTOR, RETAIL MERCHANTS' INSTITUTE

and

GRIFFIN M. LOVELACE

THIRD VICE-PRESIDENT, NEW YORK LIFE INSURANCE COMPANY
FORMERLY: DIRECTOR, LIFE INSURANCE TRAINING COURSE,
NEW YORK UNIVERSITY
DIRECTOR, LIFE INSURANCE SCHOOL OF SALESMANSHIP
CARNEGIE INSTITUTE OF TECHNOLOGY, PITTSBURGH, PA.

Assisted by

I.C.S. STAFF

ESSENTIALS OF MODERN SALESMANSHIP
MENTAL EFFICIENCY
PHYSICAL EFFICIENCY

INSTITUTE OF BUSINESS SCIENCE
SCRANTON, PA.

INTERNATIONAL TEXTBOOK PRESS
Scranton, Pa.   92004

General Summary of the Contents of
Six Books Entitled
SALESMANSHIP

BOOK I

Essentials of Modern Salesmanship

Characteristics of modern salesmanship; Old and new salesmen contrasted; Salesmanship a profession; Creative salesmanship; Qualifications and rewards of salesmen; Advantage of salesmanship; Salesmanship as a stepping-stone; Demand for salesmen; Methods of learning salesmanship.

Mental Efficiency

Personality analyzed; Importance of personality in selling work; How to develop a forceful personality; Elements of forceful personality; Imagination; Observation; Ambition; Energy; Self-confidence; Enthusiasm; Optimism; Courtesy; Tact; Self-control; Judgment; Integrity; The will; Habit; Memory; Ability to talk; The art of tactful persuasion; Good English; Using the voice effectively.

Physical Efficiency

Factors of good health; Breathing; Eating; Drinking; Bathing; Exercise; Rest and relaxation; Keeping well in warm weather; Keeping well in winter; Importance of appropriate dress; Details of appropriate dress; Miscellaneous points about appearance.

BOOK II

Study of the Customer

Buying motives; How instincts govern action; The principal instincts; Curiosity; The handling instinct; Gregariousness; The leadership instinct; Submissive instinct; Approbativeness; Acquisitive instinct; Instinct to make a profit; Instinct to secure the necessities of life; Parental instinct; Sex instincts; Fighting instinct; Play instinct; How habits differ from instincts; How to appeal to habits; Some common types of people; The indifferent buyer; The cautious buyer; The gruff customer; The argumentative customer; The cold customer; The procrastinating customer; The obstinate or prejudiced customer; The shrewd customer; The egotist; The woman buyer.

Study of the Commodity

Why the salesman should know his commodity; Preparing an analysis of selling points; Where and how to get information; Tearing the goods apart; Question method of gaining information; Factory visits; Sales manuals; Courses of instruction; Views and questions of prospective buyers, The sales manager; Experiences of other salesmen; How to make an analysis; Specimen analyses; Using the analysis.

iii

BOOK III

Beginning the Sale

The analysis of the sale; The importance of preapproach; Examples of thorough preapproach; Locating prospects; Securing information about prospects; Arranging the interview; Methods of gaining attention; Essentials of a successful approach; Preliminary size-up; Using a card; The handshake; Meeting discourtesy; Examples of successful approach; Special approaches for various commodities.

The Presentation, and Closing the Sale

How to arouse genuine interest; Service appeal; Need of thorough knowledge; Connecting Proposition with prospect's interest; Use of samples; How to use testimonials; Value of demonstrations; Demonstrating intangible commodities; Rules of demonstration; Examples of effective demonstrations; Arousing desire; Building up attractive mental pictures; Overcoming conflicting ideas; Examples of vivid word pictures. Effective closing tactics; When to close; Closing with the indecisive prospect; When postponement may be advisable; Inducements to close; Keeping customers satisfied.

BOOK IV

The Sales Talk

Necessity and methods of preparing; Memorizing the selling talk; Writing and digesting the sales talk; Writing a skeleton outline; Elimination of doubtful points; General principles of arrangement; Essential qualities of sales talk; Direction; Structure; Force. Common forms and methods of arguments; Specimen sales talks.

The Salesman's Language

Acquiring an effective style of expression; The salesman's need of good diction; Increasing the vocabulary; The dictionary habit; Essentials of good English; Clearness; Force; Harmony; Rules of capitalization; Rules for punctuation; Common errors alphabetically arranged.

BOOK V

Meeting Sales Objections

Kinds of objections; Real objections; Imaginary objections; Excuses; Methods of meeting objections; Direct rebuttal or "head-on-collision" method; The "admission-but" method; The boomerang method; Avoiding the objection; Anticipating objections; Answer to objections must appeal to customer; Objections for self-defense; Typical answers to objections.

Argument and Suggestion in Salesmanship

Argument and suggestion analyzed; Deliberation; When to use argument; How to use argument; The use of suggestion; Characteristics of suggestion; Examples of the dynamic force of suggestion; Imitation the basis of suggestion; How to use suggestion effectively; Positive suggestion; Repetition strengthens suggestions; Suggestible persons; Various applications of suggestion; Suggestion in overcoming obstacles; Suggestive value of goods and other tangible things; Suggestive value of timeliness, make, location, etc.

BOOK VI

Sales Management

The sales manager and his work; Selection of salesmen; Sources from which salesmen may be secured; Methods of selection; Training salesmen; Principal methods of training; Some distinctive methods of training; When and where to hold a sales convention; Purpose of sales contests; Elements of successful contests; Some feasible ideas for contests; What a manual should include. The salesman's equipment; Saving the salesman's time; Salesmen's compensation; Four principal forms of compensation; Some important principles of compensation.

How to Sell Your Services

Methods of finding employment; Personal qualifications; Plan your campaign; Letters of application; Answering advertisements; Direct-mail campaign; The interview; Application blanks.

CONTENTS

Book I—Salesmanship

NOTE.—This volume is made up of a number of separate parts, or sections, as indicated by their titles, and the page numbers of each usually begin with 1. In this list of contents the titles of the parts are given in the order in which they appear in the book, and under each title is a full synopsis of the subjects treated.

ESSENTIALS OF MODERN SALESMANSHIP
Serial 5084   Edition 1

	Pages
Importance of Salesmanship	1– 2
Distribution of Goods	3– 4
Characteristics of Modern Salesmanship	5–12
Old and new salesmen contrasted; Changes in selling policy; Is salesmanship a science or an art; Creative salesmanship.	
Qualifications of Salesmen	13–19
Self-development; Knowledge of the customer; Knowledge of the commodity; Details of the sale.	
Advantages of Salesmanship	20–22
Salesmanship as a stepping-stone; Demand for salesmen.	
Study of Salesmanship	23–24
The natural born salesman; Methods of learning salesmanship.	

MENTAL EFFICIENCY, PART 1
Serial 5085A   Edition 1

Personality Analyzed	1– 6
How to Develop a Forceful Personality	7–39
Elements of Forceful Personality	9–39
Imagination; Initiative, and judgment; Observation; Ambition; Energy; Self-confidence; Enthusiasm; Optimism; Courtesy; Tact; Self-control; Judgment; Integrity.	
Some Types That Lack Integrity	36–39
The guesser; The excuse maker; The loafer; The liar.	

vii

MENTAL EFFICIENCY, PART 2

Serial 5085B   Edition 1

Pages

The Will.......................................   1– 9

What the will is; Value of a well-trained will· Elements of
will power; Some things to avoid.

Habit... 10–14

Influence of habit; Importance of useful mental habits;
Maxims of habit; Franklin's method of habit formation.

Memory.. 15–25

Importance of a good memory; Fundamental principles;
Attention; Repetition; Association; Accuracy of memory;
Points to observe in memory training.

Ability to Talk............................... 26–36

Good general knowledge; Considering the listener's viewpoint; The art of tactful persuasion; Importance of correct
speech; Value of a pleasing voice; How to develop the
voice.

PHYSICAL EFFICIENCY

Serial 5087   Edition 1

Factors of Good Health........................   1–22

Proper breathing; Proper eating; Proper drinking; Proper
bathing; Exercise; Rest and relaxation; Keeping well in
warm weather; Keeping well in winter; Use of stimulants.

Details of Appropriate Dress.................. 23–33

Suits; Overcoats, hats, shirts, neckwear, and shoes; Miscellaneous points about appearance.

ESSENTIALS OF MODERN SALESMANSHIP

SELLING AS A BUSINESS FORCE

IMPORTANCE OF SALESMANSHIP

1. The window at which these lines are being written commands a view of New York harbor and the great buildings on the lower end of Manhattan Island. This view is a great moving picture, suggestive of the business of the world. Barges pass to and fro bearing railroad freight cars filled with farm and factory products, some to be loaded on ships for foreign countries, others on their way from trans-Atlantic vessels to the railroad terminals, whence they will be shipped north, south, east, and west. Powerful little tugs scurry through the channel to tow barges from dock to dock, or to help ocean-going vessels to enter or leave their piers in safety. From time to time giant steamships with huge smoke-stacks pass the Statue of Liberty headed for some European port.

In the background is the largest group of office buildings in the world. One of them alone houses about 10,000 men and women during the day; deserted at night, it opens its doors to receive them in the morning. The streets in lower Manhattan are as quiet at night as the streets of a village; but from nine o'clock in the morning until five P. M. they are crowded with hurrying, earnest throngs of people whose homes are all miles away.

It is business that keeps the harbor alive, business that attracts the great crowds daily from their distant homes, business that inspired the erection of these great sky-scrapers, 20 stories or more high.

Business is the vast organized system by which the varied wants of the human race are provided for. Goods must be produced and delivered to the men, women, and children of every community, in order that they may have the necessities of life and the many other things that contribute to their comfort and happiness.

In a mountain village of Montana or British Columbia a child is sent to buy a pound of coffee in the little store. It seems such a simple thing to do to walk into the store and ask for a pound of coffee. But if we trace this little bag of coffee back to its original source we shall be amazed that it can be bought so cheap, considering the number of people who have had a hand in its production, preparation for use, transportation and final delivery.

In South America someone cleared the land on which it grew, and purchased implements to till the soil, peasants ploughed the furrows, planted the seed, cultivated the up-springing plants, and harvested the pods; others shelled the beans and cured them, and they were packed in bags, sold to merchants, hauled to the railroad which carried them to a seaport, where they probably changed hands again and were shipped to a New York coffee firm. In New York the coffee was sold to someone who roasted and packed it whole or ground, in tins or paper bags or boxes. Wholesalers and jobbers in various cities purchased the finished product and sold it to retail customers. Steamboats, railroads, motor trucks, and horse-drawn wagons were used to transport the coffee from place to place. A pack-mule finally carried the supply that was destined to be used in the mountain village.

The miner in his humble cottage in Montana or British Columbia is able to drink his favorite beverage only because many people have cooperated in the production and distribution of coffee.

Business is concerned with preparing and distributing to consumers throughout the world the things they need or want. Capitalists, manufacturers, farmers, artisans, laborers, mechanics, railroad and steamship men, merchants, and salesmen all play a part in the production and distribution of goods.

Distribution involves merchandising and transportation; and one of the most important of all the processes of merchandising is the selling of goods by the producer, the wholesaler, and the retailer until they have ultimately been purchased by the consumer, for whose use they were originally destined. In most cases, certain persons are specially assigned to the selling of goods or services; they are called salesmen, and their work is an essential link in the business chain by which the producer and the consumer, though they dwell thousands of miles apart, are brought together.

Selling is one of the greatest of all the forces in business. It is one of the three indispensable links—production, selling, transportation—in the business chain. Unless goods are sold, the producer has worked in vain, and there is no need for transportation.

DISTRIBUTION OF GOODS

2. Successful manufacturers agree that it is easier to produce goods than to sell them; that is, the profitable sale of a new article is usually a more difficult undertaking than its manufacture. Distribution, the process of getting the product from the maker to the ultimate consumer, is therefore one of the greatest problems of the business world, since the success of a business depends ultimately on the effectiveness of the distribution of the product.

The familiar saying, "The world will beat a track to the door of the man who makes the best mouse trap, though he lives in a wilderness," is not to be taken literally; the philosopher neglected to add, "if the mouse traps are brought to the attention of those who need them." Generally speaking, to be sold successfully, goods must be meritorious, but the long list of manufacturers of meritorious goods, and dealers in them, who have failed to build up a successful business, demonstrates that in this complex age the handling of the product after it is made plays the largest part in the success of the product.

It might seem to be natural for man to know his wants or needs and to make them known to those who have the goods or service to supply such wants or needs. But products are of such a great variety and an individual's knowledge of them is necessarily so limited, that it becomes necessary to inform the public in regard to the benefits and uses of various commodities and to persuade people to buy. A retailer might profitably sell certain goods that he could order voluntarily, but often he remains unaware of the fact until he is solicited by a salesman. A farmer may be able to make profitable use of a gasoline engine, but ordinarily he will not buy until influenced by oral or printed information or solicitation.

Furthermore, human needs, instead of being fixed, are subject to constant change and development. New and improved devices are being produced continually, but they must be brought to the attention of the consuming world before there is a market for them. Thus, the salesman's field is constantly broadened and his opportunities are increased. Goods known as staples, which are generally known and for which there is a regular demand, move in the world's market with a minimum amount of sales effort. Man must have food, clothing, etc., to meet his ordinary needs; the only question is what kind of food or clothing he will buy. Yet each merchant or manufacturer must, through the salesman, secure his share of the business. Luxuries and new commodities demand more sales effort. But time moves swiftly, and the luxury or the novelty of one year may be a staple in the next. At one time, oranges were considered a luxury; they have long been staple. Grapefruit was, until recently, a novelty, and a luxury; now it may fairly be called a staple. The automobile, but a very few years ago merely an experiment, is now a necessity—a staple. Something that was needed a decade ago may not be required at all now; a new need may have replaced the old, and likewise new goods have taken the place of the old. An attractive new article, like the vacuum bottle, which keeps hot liquids hot for 2 days and cold liquids cold for 3 days, frequently comes on the market. Although it may fill a real need, there is no opportunity for the need to be definitely realized as the consumer does not know before its appearance that such an article is a possibility. But when the article appears, thousands of people are instantly attracted by it, and become owners of it, through the efforts of salesmen.

CHARACTERISTICS OF MODERN SALESMANSHIP

OLD AND NEW SALESMEN CONTRASTED

3. There is a great difference between the salesman of years ago and the trained salesman of today. The old-time drummer depended a great deal on his genial disposition and his ability to entertain his prospects with his limitless store of stories. After spinning a few yarns he was ready to sign up his prospect but without much regard to the usefulness or adaptability of the goods to the prospect's needs. The thought uppermost in his mind was *why he wanted to sell,* rather than *why his prospect should buy.* He continually thought of what he would get out of the sale—his own advantage, profits, and gains—and lost sight of what the prospect would get out of the transaction. If the order was not forthcoming he was ready to offer bribes in the form of luncheons, dinners, and shows. In fact, in some instances, he did not hesitate to use cash bribes. Getting the name on the dotted line was considered the acid test of real salesmanship, so he might even coax, beg, cajole, urge, browbeat, or use any method, short of assault, in order to close the sale.

An employer who would scoff at the idea of putting an expensive piece of machinery in the hands of an untrained man, would not hesitate to send an untrained salesman on the road to sell his merchandise. He would consider it sufficient to give him a sample case, and a few cards of the firm, with the salesman's name in the corner, and start him out with the hope that he had it in him to make good. If not, he could return discouraged and disheartened and take up inside work.

In every other branch of business the employes were supposed to be trained, but there was no time nor place for a

study of the art and science of the profession of salesmanship. Following such haphazard methods naturally meant
many failures. In fact, it is surprising that even a few were
successful by using such selfish methods in salesmanship. But
think how much more success these men could have attained,
and how much higher their self-respect would have been, had
they made a scientific study of their profession and sold from
the standpoint of sincere interest in their prospects.

The jovial salesman is still welcome today, but owing to
the new order of things, he combines a genial disposition with
a thorough knowledge of his profession. He has, through
a course of training, developed his mental ability; and his
success lies not in entertaining his prospects nor in browbeat-
ing them to get their orders, but in showing how they will
be benefited, how the goods will add to their comfort, convenience, or profit. In addition to having a course of instruction in the basic principles of selling, the modern salesman
is usually under the supervision of a competent sales manager,
who instructs him in the nature and quality of the goods and
in the meeting of the objections that are sure to arise, and
keeps him informed on all details applying to his specific line,
all of which shows that salesmanship is now a skilled profession, not a trade learned from experience alone.

CHANGES IN SELLING POLICY

4. Former Policy.—With the development of modern
salesmanship a notable change has taken place in the methods
of merchandising, and particularly in the retail field. In the
old days, the attitude of the salesman toward the customer
was concisely expressed in the phrase, "Caveat emptor" (the
Latin for "Let the buyer beware"). The purpose of the
seller was to make a profit at all hazards. The one-price
concern was a rarity. Secret price marks were used and it
was well understood that the first price asked was probably
higher than that really expected. It was taken for granted
that customer and sales person would dicker and bargain until
a satisfactory price was agreed upon. Naturally, the most

successful sales person was the one who could drive the sharpest bargain and get the most for the goods. Exchanges and credits were seldom granted, and then very grudgingly. When the customer had actually purchased the merchandise, the transaction was regarded as definitely closed. If the articles bought were not satisfactory, that was the buyer's misfortune, but an incident that imposed no obligation upon the salesman. Shopping under this system was serious business and demanded considerable caution, sagacity, and knowledge of the merchandise or proposition examined. To be sure, there were many honest business men, and many concerns that offered fair values, but the practices of the trade were such that haggling over price and standing by the bargain once made, were accepted as a matter of course by the great majority.

5. Modern Policy.—Today, every reputable concern makes only one price to each and every customer for the same grade of goods. The hard-bargaining shopper, intent on shaving the price first quoted, is usually told by the sales person with dignity, courtesy, and some pride, "This is a one-price house; we make no reductions." Moreover, exchanges and returns are freely allowed. The policy and practice today is to make it as easy and as pleasant as possible for customers to satisfy their needs. When John Wanamaker began this policy in a large way nearly a half century ago, his failure was freely predicted. But success came instead and before long his competitors were forced to imitate his example. Today all merchants are liberal in allowing customers to exchange goods, for "Satisfaction to the Customer" is a universal axiom. This may seem like altruism rather than trade, but experience has demonstrated it to be good business none the less. It is a far-sighted policy. The petty losses of today are more than offset by continued patronage from satisfied customers tomorrow and on many succeeding days. A hard-fisted, grudging policy in the handling of complaints will mean restricted business and slow growth. Adam Smith's famous phrase, the "haggling of the market," finds little application in modern selling practice.

K S F—2

The features that distinguish one concern from its competitors, that give it individuality, that make it stand for something distinctive and characteristic in the mind of the buying public, are the features of its service that excel those of its rivals. Well-trained salesmen give good service to the customer and attend to his wants in such a way that he is pleased and comes back for more goods. Concerns that are competing for business must recognize the value of securing trained salesmen. Increasingly, profits are coming to depend on the efficiency of the selling organization. The public must be attracted not merely by the advertising of the goods themselves, but by the assurance and maintenance of fair, intelligent, and even liberal treatment.

SALESMANSHIP A PROFESSION

6. During recent years salesmanship has achieved, in the opinion of some authorities, the dignity of a profession. By a profession we mean a vocation, preparation for which requires a special education, and the practice of which implies mental effort and a high plane of service. Increasingly from year to year the requirements of this definition are being satisfied by salesmanship. The need of specialized training as a basis for successful selling is clearly seen, and in various ways this need is being met. It is also recognized that salesmanship is primarily a mental operation; as one writer puts it, "Every sale is made first in the mind of the buyer." In other words, when a salesman makes a sale he does so by leading the mind of his customer to accept his proposition.

Most important of all the qualities that are associated with the term *profession* is the spirit of service, and it is this spirit that is one of the outstanding characteristics of modern selling methods.

SPIRIT OF SERVICE

7. The very heart of successful salesmanship is the clear, deliberate intention in the mind of the salesman to render the greatest possible service to every prospect. The first thought in a salesman's mind should be the determination to serve every prospect as he himself would want to be served, and by no other means can he be permanently successful. He should place himself in the position of the prospect and conscientiously do by him what he would want him to do, were their positions reversed. The salesman should consider the prospect's interests; sell to him only that which he can use, and which will prove satisfactory to him. He should prevent him from buying something he should not buy, and assist him with his judgment and experience. A real salesman will do all these things for his prospect, and while doing them he will be rendering the best service to his organization and increasing his own bank account.

A name for honesty, integrity, and character in dealing with men, is the most valuable business asset any salesman can possibly possess. A satisfied customer will pass on to his friends his favorable opinion of the good service rendered by a conscientious salesman, whose reputation will travel farther than he realizes, bringing to him customers and prospects from unexpected sources. A salesman working upon the principle that a satisfied customer is the acid test of his salesmanship, will never unduly urge a person to buy what he knows that person does not want, or cannot use, or pay for, or what would prove disappointing and unsatisfactory. He will never overstate the merits of his proposition, never leave untold anything that in common honesty, should be told, never take money for himself or his organization without conscientiously believing that he is giving value received in return. To be sure, this is a high ideal for salesmanship, but it is no higher than the highest ideal of modern business.

The salesman must become an expert in this line. He must be able to advise intelligently every prospect what to buy. To do this he must be able to analyze rightly the needs of his prospects and be able to determine the exact needs indicated by this analysis. If after a careful study of the needs of the prospect, the salesman finds that he has nothing that just suits this particular case, he will refuse to sell the prospect "something just as good," but will advise him where he can get what he needs, if he knows. He will be especially careful to set forth the details of his proposition in language so clear that there will be no possibility of misunderstanding on the part of the prospect. Any salesman whose work is based upon these high ideals will create for himself and his organization a confidence and good-will on the part of the public that will be a valuable business asset.

8. Science and Art Defined.—Until the last few decades little attention was given to the study of salesmanship as a science, though selling is one of the oldest of the arts, and has been practiced for thousands of years.

The science of any work is the collection of laws and principles that govern that work, or, as Herbert Spencer defines it, "Science is knowledge organized and systematized." Art is the ability to apply these principles and laws. To put it briefly, science is the knowing, art is the doing. Let us think, then, of salesmanship as the science that underlies the art of successful selling.

A man may have the art of doing many things with a considerable degree of skill, and at the same time he may know little or nothing of the scientific principles governing the methods he uses. For example, a plumber may have learned from experience that pipes must be arranged in certain ways to regulate the flow of air and the rise of water, but he may not know the exact laws of nature governing these matters as they have been determined by scientific investigators. On the other hand, one might understand these laws and yet be unable to apply them.

9. Acquisition of Art.—Almost any one of fair intelligence can, with a little observation and experience, learn something of the art of selling, and considerable aptitude and experience should result in more than ordinary ability, even though the science of selling is not studied in an orderly way. But the demands of modern commerce are too strong for the continuation of the plan of learning only by experience. While experience is a good teacher, it is often a slow and costly one. It is no longer advisable to attempt learning a profession solely by experience. The time has passed for learning law or medicine by obtaining a position in a lawyer's or a doctor's office and then reading his books, but depending mostly on observation and practice. The same change of procedure is taking place with respect to other professions·

10. Acquisition of Science.—Admitting all that may be claimed as to the value of learning by experience, there is no good argument for learning only by this method. It is to one's advantage, no matter how much he may be learning from experience, to gain an understanding of every law or principle that has proved of value in that line of work. In fact, no worker grows in skill only by his own efforts; he acquires some of the science of his work by watching others and by having them tell him the right and wrong way of doing things and the reasons therefor. It is therefore, much better to acquire this science in an orderly fashion than in a haphazard manner. If a man can successfully practice an art while understanding only a little of its science, he will practice it with greater certainty and success if he has a thorough knowledge of its science.

11. Need of Scientific Salesmanship.—It is hardly putting it too strongly to say that today the chief concern of the civilized nation is its commerce. The savages who traded shells or brightly colored trinkets for other things knew something of the art of selling, or exchanging; their methods, though, were governed partly by instinct and partly by experience. As exchanging was of very little importance in their lives, there was no need of their making a study of the science of selling, even if they could have undertaken such study intelligently. But the exchanging of merchandise grew in importance and volume as civilization advanced, and history shows that the ancients, whether they knew much or little of the science of their work, certainly knew much of the art of selling. The Jews, for example, have for centuries been famous as merchants.   In the last century, manufacturing has progressed by leaps and bounds.   The great strides in communication and transportation have made it easier for the Massachusetts manufacturer to sell his shoes in Texas today than it was to sell them in Pennsylvania in earlier days. Business science, in all of its branches, is better understood. Competition is keener.   Standards of efficiency are higher. What was considered fair efficiency in the art of selling 25 years ago is not up to the present standard.   To be successful, the modern salesman must be thoroughly versed in the science as well as in the art of his profession.

CREATIVE SALESMANSHIP

12.   Those who sell may be divided into two classes.   One class, undoubtedly the larger, includes those who practice the art of selling in a routine way, satisfying the needs of those buyers who know what they want, go where it is offered for sale, and ask for it.   Salesmen of this sort are merely order takers.   They really do not deserve to be called salesmen, for their duties are merely clerical, and while their selling work meets the simplest needs, it dooms a business to failure when brought into competition with more modern methods.

The modern type of salesmanship is represented by the other class of salesman—*the creative salesman.*   He realizes that he has an important mission in life to perform, and therefore he goes about his business with an enthusiasm that appeals to prospective purchasers with whom he comes into contact.   Creative salesmanship consists in making people see their needs.   This is what a well-known sales manager had in mind when he defined salesmanship as making people want what they already need.   A good salesman is like a good cook; he can create an appetite if the prospective buyer is not hungry.

The creative salesman builds business by pointing out to customers the ways in which his commodity will give them increased satisfaction, will make their lives more healthful, comfortable, or happy.   He expounds the virtues of his proposition in terms of the customers' needs and desires, so as to make them see how they may benefit by using it. Comparatively few life-insurance policies are sold as the result of men's seeking life insurance, yet creative salesmanship has caused millions of men to see the wisdom of protecting their wives and children.

Natural demand would have sold very few cash registers or adding machines; these modern and useful products owe their great success to the creative salesmanship that made men see that cash registers and adding machines increase business efficiency, and eliminate much drudgery. A famous sales manager says of cash registers: "Most of them are sold; few are bought." It is only by exploiting such machines energetically and selling a large number that the manufacturers are able to sell the machines at a reasonable cost. If sales were to be confined to hundreds instead of thousands, the cost of such machines would be prohibitive to the average buyer. Therefore, instead of selling effort adding to cost, it is actually indispensable in order that sales can be made in numbers that permit a popular or reasonable price.

Even the sales of staples are increased by creative selling effort, as is shown in the case of Domino Sugar, Uneeda Biscuit, etc., which are merely staple goods, put up in an attractive form that adds to convenience or pleasure. In these instances, it may be said that creative salesmanship which increases the demand for a commodity is a service to the public.

QUALIFICATIONS AND REWARDS OF SALESMEN

QUALIFICATIONS OF SALESMEN

13. Basis of Qualifications.—In every sale there are four factors: the salesman, the customer, the commodity (that which is sold), and the details of the sales process. The essential qualifications of a successful salesman are most conveniently grouped in four divisions based on these four factors. These divisions are: (1) Self-development; (2)

knowledge of the customer; (3) knowledge of the commodity; (4) the details of the sale.

14. Self-Development. — By self-development is meant the improvement of all the qualities that go to make up a well-rounded personality. Self-development is an important part of the training of a salesman. This is proved by the fact that in lists prepared by various authorities on salesmanship showing the essential qualities of a good salesman most of the qualities enumerated have to do with the personality of the salesman.

A list prepared by one of the best-known American sales managers names only ten qualities: Health, honesty, ability, initiative, tact, enthusiasm, sincerity, energy, open-mindedness, knowledge of business. He comments on the fact that nine of the essentials deal with the man himself and only one with the business. "This," says he, "goes to show that selling is nine-tenths man and one-tenth business."

Personality is not easy to define. It has been aptly described as that "come-hitherness" that some people have about them. This definition is excellent in that it emphasizes the importance of attractiveness in the make-up of a strong personality. But there is more than mere attractiveness in a well-developed personality. Perhaps the best way to define personality, is to say that it is a combination of positive qualities, which go to make up a character that we instinctively like, admire, and trust.

Without a pleasing and forceful personality a salesman is greatly handicapped; with it, he can easily and quickly establish satisfactory relations with those whom he canvasses, and can make himself a master of men, able to match wits with forceful characters, and to handle many a difficult situation with success.

In considering personality, it is well to remember that it is threefold in nature: (1) physical, (2) mental, and (3) moral. In planning, therefore, to build up a well-rounded personality it is necessary to give attention to each of these sides of one's make-up. The first step in the program of a practical plan of self-development is to make a list of the characteristics embodied in a complete personality. Then, using this list in a careful self-analysis the salesman should learn what traits need to be strengthened, and he should proceed to carry out a definite program of self-improvement.

Competition in the selling field has become so intense, and the life of the salesman is so strenuous that the salesman who does not make the most of his opportunities for self-growth is limiting his chances of advancement. Only the man who carefully searches for the weak points in his personality and endeavors to eradicate them by painstaking and persistent discipline can hope to number himself among the leaders in the field of selling.

15. Knowledge of the Customer.—The next essential qualification is knowledge of the customer. No study is of more importance to a salesman than that of human nature. The more he knows of his customers, the better he is prepared to know just what to do and say, in order to impress them with his goods and so make sales. Customers should be properly met and properly handled in order to attain the greatest success. While human nature is much alike everywhere, there is enough difference to make it necessary for the salesman to study the individual prospect closely. What will bring results with one might not even make an impression on another. Thus the salesman must make a close study of human nature so that he will be able to adapt himself quickly to each prospect he will meet.

Many people are of the opinion that the characteristics of a person can be detected by the shape and measurement of the head itself, the forehead and eyes, lips, chin, etc. Phrenology is not, however, a fruitful subject of study for salesmen, as they lack the time needed to go thoroughly into the subject. In the quick action required for salesmanship, there is not time for such work. The salesman may have a few minutes to study the face and he may, possibly, hear the prospect say a few words; out of this material he must form his estimate of the man with whom he is to deal.

Nature has given man a certain perceptive sense—a sixth sense, so to speak. The child, even before it can talk, seems able to tell, from people's faces, whether or not they like children. When a man enters a barber shop and three or four barbers go to their chairs, he takes a swift glance at them. One face makes a better impression than another and the customer walks to that barber's chair. He may not be able to say what kind of head the barber he selected has, nor tell the color of his eyes; he only knows that he has the general impression that the barber is a careful man.

Much of the first impression depends on the spoken word. The gruff voice, the sharp or nervous voice, and the pleasant, deliberate voice convey messages to the mind of the discerning salesman and enable him to measure swiftly his prospect. It is impossible for a salesman to understand how to proceed with certain people until he has had an opportunity to hear them speak and discuss matters.

The environment of the prospect often furnishes some helpful information. The condition of his store or desk, farm or buildings, the kind of equipment with which he works, the pictures on the wall, etc., all reflect his attitude of mind, whether orderly or slovenly, progressive or conservative, practical or imaginative, liberal or penurious, and furnish valuable hints as to his disposition and his habits.

Then there are other outward signs which reveal a person's character and act as a guide to the salesman in presenting his arguments. These are evidenced in the walk, clothes, actions, etc. In order to size up a customer a salesman must school himself diligently in the study of human nature. Especially important is it for him to understand the instincts that control people's actions, for by observing what instincts are predominant he can so shape his selling argument as to appeal to those instincts and thus make easy the winning of sales.

16. Knowledge of the Commodity.—Every day thousands of sales are lost because salesmen are unfamiliar with the merits of what they are selling. A salesman may not possess all the qualifications that are necessary for success in selling, but if he has a thorough knowledge of his commodity, he possesses three-fourths of the necessary qualifications for making the sale. On the other hand, a salesman who does not know his commodity and who attempts to win sales by general statements is sure to be embarrassed sooner or later by the questions offered by some prospect who possesses a definite knowledge of the commodity.

An incident is related of a salesman who was considered one of the best in his line. He seemed to be able to handle successfully selling propositions that involved considerable technical detail, and yet he made no effort to conceal the fact that his knowledge of his commodity included nothing but a few superficial details and the price. The success of this man was due to his consummate ability to handle skilfully the various types of human nature with which he came in contact. He relied upon this ability, an unusual fund of information, and a most magnetic personality to achieve results which would have been greatly multiplied, had he fully equipped himself by becoming familiar with the merits of his commodity.

The advantages to the salesman of knowing his commodity are numerous. In the first place, a thorough knowledge of the commodity adds interest to his work and takes the drudgery out of it. The natural result of a thorough knowledge of anything worth while is to develop enthusiasm about it. Enthusiasm is obviously a great asset to a salesman, for a salesman who can talk enthusiastically about the merits of his commodity is more easily able to convince his prospects and close his sales than is the salesman whose incomplete knowledge make his sales talk perfunctory and lifeless.

The second advantage of knowing all that is possible about a commodity is that thorough knowledge develops in the salesman self-confidence, without which he can hardly expect to cope successfully with the forceful personalities with which his selling work necessarily brings him in touch. This self-confidence on the part of the sales person impresses those whom he faces and is reflected sooner or later in their confidence in both the salesman and what he is selling. Because permanent business relations are based upon confidence, anything that tends to develop this asset should be recognized at its true value and should be developed to the utmost.

One of the most important functions of the salesman is that of acting as an expert adviser to his customers. If he has a thorough knowledge of what he is selling, he will be able to judge the adaptability of his commodity to the needs of his customers and thereby he will be able to serve his customers better.

A very practical reason for the need of intimate knowledge of the commodity is that it furnishes a salesman with material for building up a selling talk that will be informing and convincing. Definite knowledge will enable the salesman to use specific statements instead of vague general claims that have no selling force. It will enable him to handle more effectively prospects that are slow about reaching a decision to buy simply because they have not yet been convinced.

Finally, complete knowledge helps the salesman to overcome a natural tendency to omit from his sales talk many important features of his commodity which he takes for granted because he thinks they are evident at a glance. It is assumed that when a prospect looks at something for sale he sees what the salesman intends he should see. But very often this is not true. People do not see what they look at; they see only that which is pointed out to them. A salesman who has worked out in his mind a complete and detailed description of what he is trying to sell will be very likely to call his prospect's attention to the things the prospect should notice. In so doing, he will greatly improve the quality of his sales talk and will increase the number of sales that he makes.

17. Details of the Sale.—Every sale is divided into four steps that indicate the stages through which the mind of the purchaser is guided by the salesman. Whether a customer is buying a newspaper or a suit of clothes, his mind passes through these different stages, though in many cases the transition from one stage to another is hardly perceptible.

The four stages of the sale are *attention, interest, desire,* and *action.* An efficient salesman needs to know how to handle effectively each of these stages. In order to attract attention he must know how to make the best possible use of his knowledge of the customer so that the first impression that he makes will be a favorable one. He must know how to concentrate the attention of the customer upon what he is selling. Sometimes a sale depends upon the first few words used by the salesman as he faces the customer, for if he cannot make a favorable impression with his opening remarks a chance to continue his selling talk will not be given him. After the salesman has succeeded in getting attention, his next task is to rouse in the mind of his customer an interest in what he is selling. To do this he must know how to present his selling points in such a way that they will make a strong appeal to the individual needs of each customer. At this stage of the sale, the salesman makes use of both his knowledge of the goods and knowledge of the customer.

Having developed an interest in his commodity, the salesman must know how to intensify this interest sufficiently to arouse in the customer a desire to possess it. He must know how to handle objections, oftentimes by answering them before they are expressed, and be able to present the distinctive merits of his commodity vividly and forcefully. He must persuade the prospect to reject opposing desires that might interfere with the purchase. He must definitely portray the advantages that will accrue to the prospect from possessing his commodity.

Until the salesman has secured from the prospect definite action, his efforts are without result. Therefore it is regarded as especially important for the salesman to be able to close a reasonable proportion of his interviews with an order. While it is true that proper handling of the preceding steps of the sale will generally make it easy to secure the final decision to buy that is the result of a successful canvass, there are many fine points in the technique of selling that have to do with methods of transforming a desire to possess into a definite decision to buy.

During the last few years much attention has been given to the proper procedure at each step of the selling process, and certain definite principles have been established with which every salesman should become familiar. He should know how to locate prospects, how to approach them effectively, and how to argue forcefully and tactfully. He should be able to make the right use of samples, to make it easy for the customer to sign an order, and to maintain friendly and profitable relations with him. Often a salesman's failure is due to his inability to handle successfully one or more of these details in the selling process.

ADVANTAGES OF SALESMANSHIP

COMPARISON WITH OTHER LINES OF BUSINESS

18. Salesmanship has many advantages over other professions and lines of business. The business man requires capital, but the salesman does not; his employer takes all risk of manufacture and sales, and pays the salesman liberally for his work. The owner of the retail business must carry a stock, which is subject to expense and the risk of non-sale, depreciation, loss by fire, etc. The salesman's stock is his ability to sell; even the samples he carries are usually furnished by his house.

The professional man requires long and arduous training, costing thousands of dollars, and he is able to earn only after he has passed collegiate and state examinations; the period of sales training is relatively brief and inexpensive and the salesman can begin to earn as soon as he can convince his employer that he can sell. The cost of a professional education in time and money is a good deal, and often, after years of arduous study, more years and money are required for building up a practice. The professional man loses standing the minute he seeks business; the salesman has no such restrictions; indeed, he is supposed to get out and create a demand for what he has to sell.

The man in the trades must not only spend a considerable time in apprenticeship, but must conform to the usual wage scale; the salesman may earn while he is learning; and his employer is glad to see him earn money, for the more the salesman earns, the more profit he makes for the house. It is far easier for the salesman to secure an increase in income than it is for the office employe; the employer is always glad to pay more to the salesman who creates business, while as a rule he is rarely willing to pay more to the inside worker, who is looked upon as an expense. Salesmen earn several times as much as workers of corresponding ability in most other positions.

The man who has learned to sell is not only secure in his ability to make money; he has acquired abilities that are regarded with admiration by others. His work gives him bearing and confidence. His training gives him the ability to bring others to his way of thinking. His constant association with opportunity gives him an optimistic outlook.

Most men are accustomed to dealing with ready-made opportunities. Not so with the creative salesman; he makes his own opportunities. And he is used to making others see opportunities. He has the knack of seeing, recognizing, and making the most of the various opportunities open to the man who constantly meets other men. No accurate record of the comparative percentage of promotions in the sales, operating, and executive departments is commonly kept. But the sales force is constantly drawn from in the promotion of men to more responsible positions.

SALESMANSHIP AS A STEPPING STONE

19. So well recognized is the value of training acquired by successful selling that, when choosing men for important positions, managers give preference to men who have at some time sold goods. They know that the man who has a record for successful selling must have the qualifications that are requisite for success in larger positions.

One reason why successful selling leads to business success is that the salesmen meet people and learn to influence them and to get along well with others. The man shut up in a narrow office or shop, where the few people he meets have no greater power than himself, is unfortunate. He may grow, but the conditions are unfavorable, for the greatest battles of life, also the opportunities, are those in which man meets man. A man is developed by his contact with other men. Mingling with successful men, seeing their methods of work, studying their personalities, and hearing their talk is of great value in the development of the well-rounded, confident, judicious, efficient business man.

Salesmanship offers a person a great opportunity to demonstrate his ability to large numbers of business men. The salesman's ability is widely observed and commented on. It is brought to the knowledge of thousands of alert business men, who are always looking for business getters. Many a man has made a profitable connection because he was able to sell to some hard-headed customer who was himself on the lookout for a salesman. Every sale advertises the ability of the salesman.

DEMAND FOR SALESMEN

20. Demand is an index to worth. The demand for capable salesmen is never fully supplied. The daily papers contain from three to ten advertisements for salesmen to one for a man wanted in any other line. Besides, every sales manager of a large business concern would be willing to add to his staff men who can show results as salesmen if he knew where to find them. Many large concerns can satisfy their needs only by establishing expensive training schools and then searching for likely men and developing them.

In the manufacturing end of a business, a manager must be fully justified by the demand before he puts in an extra machine, for this requires more power. He must carefully study the conditions before he adds another engine to the equipment, for this increases the expense of running the plant. But, as a general rule, the addition of a strong salesman to the force may be made at any time, for this means an immediate increase in the receipts. The more sales made, the greater is the amount of money coming in; consequently, the greater are the profits. As a result, good salesmen are in constant demand. There is always a lack of good business getters; they cannot be developed fast enough to supply the demand. Competitive concerns are constantly taking valuable men away from one another by paying higher salaries. Not only is this conclusive proof of the sureness and permanence of selling work from the viewpoint of the individual, but it shows how dependent modern business is on salesmanship.

STUDY OF SALESMANSHIP

21. The Natural Born Salesman.—For a long time after the importance of salesmanship as a business force was recognized it was believed that salesmanship could not be taught. The old saying, "Salesmen are born, not made" found ready acceptance, and it was thought that unless a person was born with certain talents he could not hope to become a successful salesman. Gradually it came to be realized that one born with certain talents may perfect and multiply them by systematic training. The truth of the matter is, it is easier to make a good salesman out of one not born with great natural gifts in that direction, but who will work and learn, than it is to make a truly great salesman out of one with natural gifts, who is not progressive enough to cultivate and develop those gifts.

The natural-born salesman is likely to be an unsatisfactory member of a sales force. He is prone to depend upon his natural brilliancy for results, and if they do not come easily, he often slumps in his work for days at a time, and because he has no foundation of scientific knowledge to give him courage in trying situations, his aggregate sales as a rule will be less than those of the salesman who works along scientific lines, taking all possible advantage of the lessons learned from the experience of others, and refusing to be discouraged by occasional rebuffs.

E. D. Gibbs, for many years trainer of salesmen for the National Cash Register Company, says about natural-born salesmen:

"One of the most foolish mottoes ever written was the one 'A salesman is born, not made.' It is true that some salesmen are natural-born sellers of goods. They possess a certain gift and a certain temperament which enables them to go

K S F—3

out and meet people and win their confidence, but where you find one man of this kind, you find a hundred others who do not possess this natural ability. These men must have their talents developed by competent instruction. If the great manufacturing concerns of this country waited for salesmen to be born, there would not be any goods sold. These concerns are wise enough to know that, given the necessary ability. with the proper help and right surroundings, a man can be trained to sell goods."

22. Methods of Learning Salesmanship.—At the present time, there are four principal methods of learning salesmanship: (1) Study of an orderly treatment of the science, such as is here given. (2) Study, or study and practice combined in a training school established by an employer for the special purpose of providing training in salesmanship for his particular needs. (3) Drawing on the experience of other salesmen by associating with them, going out with them on their calls, talking with them, and reading their experiences in books, magazines, etc., and by seeing demonstrations by sales managers or others. (4) Learning through experience.

The ambitious man will take advantage of the first, third, and fourth methods in any event, and will get all he can from each. The first method will give an admirable preparation for the third and fourth, because, understanding the science of his work, the salesman can keep clear of those practices that the experiences of others have shown to be inadvisable. Furthermore, he will be able to understand and apply quickly all that comes to him through experience. He will know the reason for things and can act with greater confidence. If at any time a student of salesmanship is required to adopt the second method, it will be easy work, for, having followed the first method, all that he must learn at an employer's school will be the technical details and certain preferred methods of that special business.

MEMORY HELPS

He who can answer the following questions from memory has a good understanding of the text in the preceding pages.

(1)   What are the meaning of the words *science* and *art* as used in connection with salesmanship?

(2)   Define salesmanship.

(3)   Why must the salesman understand human nature?

(4)   What facts show that salesmen are always in demand?

(5)   In what way is the natural-born salesman likely to prove unsatisfactory?

(6)   Mention some advantages salesmanship has over other professions and lines of business.

(7)   State the essential qualifications of a successful salesman.

(8)   Give four principal methods of studying salesmanship.

(9)   What is the importance in selling work of a knowledge of the commodity?

(10)   Why should a salesman study himself—his strong and weak characteristics?

(11)   What is the difference between an order taker and a creative salesman?

MENTAL EFFICIENCY
(PART 1)

PERSONALITY ANALYZED

1. Introduction.—In our study of the subject of Salesmanship we shall first give attention to the salesman, and we shall consider how the salesman may develop himself so as to attain the highest degree of success.

In the modern business world with its keen competition, man power is the greatest force. Man power is the power of intellect, will, and personality. To succeed in a large way, one must develop the ability to think straight, the will to persevere, and the power to talk and act in a way that impresses other people. The development of man power, or personality, is especially essential in the field of salesmanship, because the salesman is constantly in contact with other people, and must match wits with them. To succeed, he must develop a forceful, attractive, and well-rounded personality.

2. What is Personality?—Personality is not an easy word to define. The dictionary tells us that personality is the sum of the qualities peculiar to any person, which distinguish that person from every one else. It is a combination of the physical, mental, and moral qualities, and, therefore, contrary to what some people think, is more than appearance, or an artificial manner that can be put on at will. It is the expression of one's real self and gives a man the power to attract others, provided he has developed those physical, mental, and moral qualities that give charm, attractiveness, and forcefulness to his individuality.

Every man has a personality of some sort just as he has a brain and a body. It may be strong or weak, attractive or repulsive; but no man is without one. A weak brain or a sickly body may signify a bad personality just as bad steel or leaky cylinders spoil an engine. Similarly, faulty education may train a man's actions, expression or feelings in such a way that people will be impressed with his repelling personality.

We speak of personality as being pleasing or repellent, forceful or weak, but in its ordinary use, the term personality has a favorable meaning, so that when we say of a person, "He has *personality*," we mean that he possesses certain qualities that are pleasing or forceful, and that enable him to influence others. Let us think, then, of personality as the power possessed by a person to influence others.

3. Importance of Personality in Selling Work.—Most men, if asked what determines success in selling work, would probably reply, personality. Purchasing agents and others thrown into contact with many salesmen say that they have to be constantly on guard against the tremendous force of personality. Various classes of goods practically sell themselves, so that into the sale of these it is not necessary to introduce strong personality; but wherever it is necessary to educate the prospective buyer as to the need or the usefulness of the article, or wherever competition is strong, the force of the salesman's personality is frequently a greater factor in making a sale than the merits of the commodity.

Real salesmanship is a meeting of minds, in which the salesman's mind succeeds in inducing the other mind to look upon the commodity under discussion as it exists in the mind of the salesman. If the mind were a mere machine that could weigh all evidence for and against a proposition and show which side had the better argument, personality would count for but little. But just as the personality of the minister may greatly affect his message and his audience, and the personality of the lawyer may sway a jury, so the personality of the salesman, if properly developed, may strongly influence his hearer, the customer.

4. Physical Personality.—Personality is three-fold in nature: (1) Physical; (2) mental; (3) moral. In order to possess a well-rounded personality it is absolutely necessary to develop each of these.

The physical is the element first noticed in the individual; the man of commanding size and well-proportioned form attracts attention by these qualities alone. Every movement, action, and manner, every handshake, every smile, and every word is a part of this same visible personality. Business men are often heard to remark that they cannot shake hands effectively; but it is noticed that it does not require long for the raw country boy to learn to salute his superiors after he has enlisted in the army—because they know how to teach him how it is done. The improved military bearing of the young soldier becomes a part of his personality. It makes him more effective in his contacts with people. It would be just as easy for the salesman to improve himself in his physical personality as it is for the recruit to acquire his military carriage, if there were some one to tell him what he lacked and what to do to correct his deficiency. Any one who will carefully analyze persons that have attractive physical personalities and then study himself, can easily learn what he lacks and can, in time, by earnest and persistent effort greatly improve himself in this regard.

We have mentioned size as a factor contributing to the physical personality. Yet large stature is not necessary to a strong personality. In fact, the man who has the large form and lacks some of the finer qualities may even be repulsive rather than attractive, whereas on the other hand we often meet people of small stature and inferior natural appearance, who are exceptionally winning and magnetic, because they possess other desirable qualities so highly developed as to offset their lack of an imposing figure. The basis of the physical personality is health. In order to reach his highest effectiveness, the salesman must have an abundant store of vital energy and must keep himself at all times in good physical condition. The factors that underlie good health are discussed in detail in a later Section.

5. Mental Personality.—The mental side of personality is not so easily understood as the physical, but it is just as important, as it is the power back of the physical. It has been known for centuries that the thought determined the man. More than 3,000 years ago a very wise philosopher said, "As a man thinketh in his heart so is he," and the generations since have seen this statement verified. We know that thoughts are forces in that they cause physical action. We know that we are what our thoughts have made us.

It is difficult to realize the fact that our whole personality is due in a very large measure to what we think. It is so easy to believe that we are as we are by accident, that we do not consider seriously the possibility of remolding our personalities by occupying our minds with the right kind of thoughts.

A simple little experiment will demonstrate the effect of thought upon the outward expression or personality. It is impossible to think a mean thought and smile at the same time. This statement may seem extreme, but a trial will convince you that it is true. Try smiling the pleasantest smile at your command. Then, holding the smile, think a mean thought, say a thought of hatred. You will feel the muscles of your face contract, and the smile will give way to a very different facial expression, unless you hold the smile by force of your will. Even if you succeed in retaining the smile by an effort of your will, you will find that the expression of your eyes will change. Just the instant the mind changes from the cheerful thought to the other, the facial expression changes, the hold is loosened on the nerves and muscles that control the smile, and there comes into your face an expression that matches the disagreeable thought within.

We see this same principle illustrated about us every day. We often meet people bowed with the weight of years and with faces seamed and furrowed, whose expression is, nevertheless, kindly and winning. We forget the wrinkles and our hearts are warmed by their smiles. And we meet others, also bowed and wrinkled, who are repulsive. The difference lies in the difference between the kind thoughts of the former and the unpleasant thoughts of the others. If one thinks mean, low, degrading thoughts for three score years, the wrinkles of the face, the cast of the eye, the action of the whole body, will reflect them.

No man can think wrong thoughts habitually without running the risk of having other people sense his state of mind, as they look at his face. Every one feels that strange, unexplainable, but distinct impression that comes from a stranger's personality at the moment of a first meeting. There is often an instantaneous feeling of like or dislike, of confidence or distrust.

In the light of these facts, we know that the person who would become attractive and develop a winning personality must cultivate his thinking, in addition to training his body in correct posture and exercising to keep it well. If, when we think of people, we think kind thoughts, we shall soon be doing kind deeds. If we think cooperation, we shall act cooperatively, helping our friends and neighbors, serving the customers well, and we shall thereby gain in personality.

The optimist and the pessimist are examples of positive and negative mental personalities. The one sees the best in every situation, the other always sees the worst. The one looks on the bright side of life. He wants to see the sunny side and does see it, because he wants to. His face, his manner, and his conversation all reflect sunshine. To the pessimist every day is gloomy, every situation full of harmful possibilities. While the optimist is full of hope, the pessimist is a messenger of despair. The one buoys us up, the other is a "kill-joy."

If you were a merchant and on a fine June morning greeted a customer with a crabbed snarl, peevishly asked what he wanted, complained about poor business, the poor town, and the mean class of people in the community, you would make the customer sorry he had entered your store. He would be glad to get away and would probably never return, if he could conveniently get what he wanted elsewhere. You would have lost a customer through an unfavorable mental personality. How much more profitable would it have been for you as a business man, and how much more pleasant for the customer if you had greeted him with a cheery "Good morning," made a remark about the glorious day, saying you were glad to see such weather. If the customer happened to be a stranger, how easy it would have been to speak a good word for your town, saying, "This is one of the best towns in the state." Such a mental attitude would have made the customer glad he had gone to your store. Both of you would have enjoyed doing business together and your customer would have felt that he wanted to come back again.

We cannot too strongly emphasize the fact that people are conscious of our mental personality, as they are aware of our physical personality. Dr. Marden says, in speaking of the mental side of personality: "Your poverty of books, of education, of reading, of travel, of experience, of sympathy, of tolerance, your wealth of thought, of splendid discipline; your fine training; your righteousness and mellowness of heart and sweetness of disposition; your bank deposit of cheerfulness, of helpfulness, and of inspiration, will be immediately apparent to every person you converse with."

6. Moral Personality.—By moral personality, we mean the contribution that is made to personality by sound character. It is, of course, intimately related to mental personality, since our thought habits are largely determined by what we actually are in terms of honesty, sincerity, courtesy, charity, forbearance, courage, generosity, perseverance, and other qualities of character.

Too much emphasis cannot be laid on the value of sound character as a factor of personality. We say, "As a man thinketh in his heart, so is he." It may also be said, with equal truth, "As a man is, so doth he think and act." Genuine personality, as contrasted with superficial personality, is the well-rounded personality that not only pleases, through physical charm and through the glow that radiates from a cheerful, optimistic, confident, sympathetic mental attitude, but also wears well, because it is the expression of sound moral qualities, or, as we commonly say, is the reflection of character.

In the development of moral personality, it is important to guard carefully against harmful environment and associations.

Adults, as well as children, are easily led to imitate others. By associating with persons of sound character, whose enjoyment lies in doing things that are elevating, rather than things that degrade, one will find it easier to control his own character-building habits.

HOW TO DEVELOP A FORCEFUL PERSONALITY

WHY PERSONALITY IS OFTEN UNDEVELOPED

7. Many people still cling to the old notion that personality cannot be developed. They claim that personality is only natural, and are content to blame Nature for their shortcomings. There are many salesmen who might be winning and magnetic were it not for this false notion. They believe that, having been born weak and unattractive, that is, with negative or repellent personalities, they cannot be different and they make no effort to improve or strengthen their personalities.

Every one has within him, in some measure, those qualities the development of which makes personality. Every one is born with the same muscles, some stronger than others. Yet even those who are physically weak can, by exercise, develop strong muscles. So, too, persons whose personalities are not naturally strong possess at least the rudiments of qualities that can be developed by training.

When a salesman sees a person of strong and winning presence he should not deplore his own short-comings, saying "How fortunate he is to be born with such magnificent faculties, and to have such a nature." On the contrary, he should analyze the personality which he admires and determine exactly in what ways this person is stronger than he is, and then set about to remedy his own weaknesses. A man should never permit himself to think he is hopelessly weak in certain traits, for the truth is that he is deficient only because he allows himself to be so.

If he goes around saying that he knows he is going to fail and that everybody else can succeed but he cannot, he is simply courting weakness and depreciating himself. The minute he depreciates himself, he diminishes his self-confidence and consequently lessens the force of his personality, for self-confidence is a decidedly important element of personality; indeed, it is one of the first requisites of success. Watch an athlete as he makes a high jump. If he runs up to the bar entertaining the idea that he cannot fulfill his purpose he actually finds himself unable to succeed in his effort or else falls short a number of inches of the height that he is physically able to leap. Let him, however, come up to the bar firm in the belief that he can clear the distance, and he will perform creditably up to the limit of his physical powers. We pity, but do not admire, the batter in the baseball game who takes his bat but remarks that he knows he is going to strike out. The moment he entertains that idea, the pitcher has won a great advantage over him. But if he goes to bat full of enthusiasm and vim, believing that he is going to place a hit so skilfully, or knock such a hot liner that no one can handle it, he has the advantage over the pitcher; his muscles and eyes are prepared to do their best.

The salesman who desires to improve his personality should make up his mind that he can develop his own personality by following the principles upon which personal strength is founded. No matter what may be his present shortcomings, he can become more forceful, winning, and magnetic, if he will make up his mind to do so.

It seems strange that the average individual gives so little thought to the subject of his own personal development when every one would like to have a pleasing personality. It is no uncommon thing to hear some one remark that he regrets his lack of personality. That same person would feel insulted were some one to tell him that he could not learn to follow a line in sawing a board, or that he could not learn to do a simple sum in mathematics. Any normal human being can learn to strengthen his personality as he can learn to do other things. For example, he can learn to talk persuasively and to be kindly and courteous. These things are important elements of an effective personality. Therefore, when one learns to talk better, to be more kindly toward others and more courteous he is developing his personality. Likewise other elements of personality can be strengthened by persistent discipline. There are millions of people who have failed to achieve success because, not being possessed of attractive personalities, they have neglected to cultivate those traits which would make them attractive to others, just as many persons, born with weak bodies, have gone through life handicapped because they have neglected to strengthen their bodies by exercise and by regular observance of the laws of right living.

ELEMENTS OF FORCEFUL PERSONALITY

SELF-ANALYSIS AIDS PERSONAL DEVELOPMENT

8. The first step for the salesman to take in developing the elements of a forceful personality is to make a detailed self-

Elements of a Forceful Personality
{
Imagination
Observation
Ambition
Energy
Self-confidence
Enthusiasm
Optimism
Courtesy
Tact
Self-control
Judgment
Integrity
Habit
Will
Memory
Ability to talk
Good health
Good appearance
}

Fig. 1

analysis, for the act of looking within himself will show him what qualities he possesses, and in what qualities he is deficient; it will also show along what lines he should endeavor to grow and what traits should be controlled.

The chart in Fig. 1 should be closely studied, for it covers the physical as well as the mental and moral qualities of a forceful personality. The following treatment of these essentials furnishes the ideas that should be put into practical use. So the salesman should go over the chart carefully and ask himself to what degree he possesses each essential, whether he is strong, medium or weak in each one. Then after determining along what lines he needs developing, he can concentrate on those needed qualities and from the suggestions given concerning them, he can select and apply those ideas which will help him most.

IMAGINATION

9. Importance of the Imagination.—Imagination is a great factor in business, and especially in selling, for it is very helpful in the solution of difficulties and in the discovery of new means to the ends that are sought. Imagination in business is the mental process of picturing familiar things in new combinations, combinations that are new to ourselves or new to the whole world. In other words, it is taking past experiences and combining them in new ways to produce new things; it is putting old material in new form. For example, George Pullman's imagination took several old ideas with which he was quite familiar and pictured them in a new combination, as a solution of the problem of the man who wanted both to travel and to sleep comfortably at night. A cushioned bench, a bed, portières, and a closet were all old ideas. But Mr. Pullman's imagination pictured two cushioned seats facing each other transformed into a bed concealed by portières, with another bed overhead folding away into a closet. The mental picture—the product of his imagination—was reproduced in a model, and as a result we have the Pullman sleeping car.

Everything new once existed in some one's imagination. Men do not create things without first having ideas, which have been carefully developed in their imaginations until the ideas have acquired the desired shape.

Cyrus W. Field worked out in his imagination a scheme of joining America and England by cable. It was a dream until finally, after repeated failures, the great cable line was laid and the dream became a famous reality.

The Wright flying machine was a dream in the brain of the Wright brothers before it became a reality. These brothers were called dreamers until their flying machine demonstrated its success; then they were called geniuses. Without imagination they would never have been able to conceive the idea of a practical airplane.

10. Application of Imagination to Selling.—Imagination is necessary to the salesman in constructing from past experiences new methods of handling different customers. As no two customers are exactly alike, the arguments must be changed and presented in many different ways to make the desired impression. The facts that memory and observation furnish should be used to build up new ideas.

When a retail salesman is dealing with a woman customer he must try to imagine from his dealing with various customers, her thoughts and emotions, her way of looking at things. He must form some mental picture, when required, of her home surroundings or of all things not present that may affect her purchase. In other words, he needs imagination to work beyond the presence of the customer, to picture her thoughts, her surroundings, her background, and all those influences that will affect her decision.

The highest-salaried salesmen are those with creative imaginations, men who can see in their imagination the persons to whom they are appealing and understand what will interest these persons, what they will want to know, etc. When the salesman has new goods to sell, he must make it his practice to imagine that he is the prospective buyer and must then ask, "Why should I buy these goods?" "Why are they better than other goods of the same class?" "What would interest and convince me?" By thus looking at the goods from the prospective purchaser's point of view, he can get at the right sales argument.

Obviously, the man without imagination is a slow plodder along the ruts that others have cut before him. He is not a creator but a good follower. An instance exemplifying this fact is cited by Lorin F. Deland. A young man, earning $12 a week in a clothing store, asked Mr. Deland how he could earn more. The former first suggested that the young man use his imagination for a month, trying to devise methods of bringing more business to the store. At the end of the month, the young man said that he could think of no plan to increase the sales of the store. He was then advised to spend a month trying to devise some means of reducing the operating expenses. When he failed to do this, also, Mr. Deland advised him to lie low, to attract as little attention to himself as possible. This young man was merely a type of many thousands who seem devoid of creative imagination.

11. Training the Imagination.—Imagination, as used in business, can be acquired, so there is no reason why a salesman should be without this quality which is so essential in efficient salesmanship. Thorough knowledge is the first requisite of imaginative power, for naturally the wider one's knowledge and the broader the field of view, the more fruitful will be the imagination. The man who reads, meets many people, and gets new experiences gives his imagination more scope, and at the same time evolves, so to speak, a balance wheel with which to regulate it. His varied experiences develop the reasoning power that not only suggests new and useful ways and means, but that may be used as a check on the imagination when its creations are too fanciful to be realized. The old admonition to get out of the rut is merely a way of saying that the imagination needs fresh material with which to work.

Nature is a powerful stimulator to the imagination. A great uplift is felt when one occasionally turns to the beauties of fields, woods, rivers, and mountains. They afford a never-ending source of profitable reflection—the kind of reflection that strengthens character. Mixing in the whirl of business is invaluable, for it rubs off the sharp corners and trims and hardens for efficient action, but a man never attains full development without being to some extent alone, where his imagination responds to the voice of nature and he communes with his best self. It is particularly important to keep undesirable thoughts out of the mind. Though they will come unbidden, every man has the power to reject evil suggestions; he is not obliged to give these thoughts full sway—to allow the imagination to build up evil pictures that must have some harmful effect. The man who permits his imagination to dwell continually on vicious things may expect his mental garden to be overrun with weeds; he can look for no better harvest. When fear, discouragement or resentment present themselves, all his powers of countersuggestion should be brought into full play, until these forerunners of defeat are replaced with confidence, courage, friendliness, and all the related qualities that give buoyancy to the mentality and stimulate the imagination to a state of healthful activity.

12.   Imagination, Initiative, and Judgment.—Imagination without initiative is as helpless as knowledge without courage, and either imagination or initiative without judgment is as useless as enthusiasm is unless it is backed up by earnest effort along definite lines. A real-estate owner put a large tract of land on the market. He called in an artist to prepare advertising copy for the sales campaign. The latter, in making a trip to the tract, found the owner slashing down trees. "Don't," cried the artist, "let me first draw the picture with all its foliage so we can call it 'Bungalow Hill.' Then you can go ahead." In the meantime the owner began putting his salesmen to work and told them to get on the job. One salesman, upon receipt of the artist's print and other literature, went out to look over the tract. Finding the tree-slashing process in full swing, he asked that it be stopped, saying, "If this is to be Bungalow Hill, leave enough trees on each lot to afford shade." He supplied the judgment that was lacking in the imaginative artist and the initiative mind of the owner. The salesman had the true sales instinct, for he saw the value of the trees as a business proposition.

K S F—4

OBSERVATION

13.   Observation is a quality that is born of alertness—of a wide-awake interest in things; and the things observed depend on where one's interest is placed.   The person who is not interested in his fellow men nor their activities, who goes through life practically asleep, gives scant attention to the things seen and heard, and needless to say, his is a humdrum existence, devoid of enjoyment or success.   But the person with a well-defined aim in life will see in the men and things about him something related to his trade, profession or hobby.   A landscape artist, in viewing an apple tree in its beautiful spring attire, will see in it the beauty of form, color, and pastoral atmosphere that he can transfer to his canvas.   The thrifty farmer may see in the same tree a harvest that will later bring coins to his purse.   In walking down a city street, an architect notices the style of architecture of the buildings, the materials of which they are made, etc.; but the physician will probably observe the amount of air and sunshine that the windows will admit to the houses, whether the sewers will carry away all the waste water, whether the streets are kept clean, and so on.

But where should the salesman's observation lie?   Perhaps no other trade or profession calls for more keen observation that covers interests so widely spread.   He cannot indulge what may be called selective observation.   There is, of course, the immediate observation of things concerned with the product he sells, and this is of much importance.   A salesman walking through the great H. J. Heinz kitchens saw that the pickles were carefully assorted as to sizes, and put into the bottles in just the same order, and that the little piece of red pepper was always inserted at the same place in each bottle.   His observation and his inquiries gave him the knowledge of the exact, careful way in which his employers did their factory work, so that he was afterwards able to use that point.

But the salesman whose observation is limited to the commodity he is selling misses seeing many things that he can use to advantage in his work.   He comes into daily contact with persons of a great variety of aims, interests, and dispositions, and to deal with them successfully his habit of observation must be cultivated to such an extent that it is ever active. He will note during an interview objects in the room, movements of the prospect, words or tones of the voice, and many other things that may help him to so shape his canvass as to make the most effective appeal to the prospect.

A salesman who had been wholly unsuccessful in getting an order from a grouchy country storekeeper, decided that he would, if possible, remain in the store long enough to find some point of contact with this reticent man, and got permission to stay there until train time, which was an hour hence. Much of this time had passed without a word passing between the storekeeper and the salesman. Then it happened that a very nice cat, in passing the storekeeper, rubbed itself gently against him. The grouchy storekeeper stooped down and petted it a trifle and went on. Here was the point of contact. Later when the cat became friendly with the salesman, who was also fond of cats, the way was open for genial conversation, and then as the salesman put it, "You should have heard Kimball on cats!" Without solicitation, the storekeeper, after some talk that became interesting and friendly, placed a substantial order.

So the salesman will do well to strengthen his power of observation. A rather mechanical but nevertheless good practice is, when passing a store window, for instance, to concentrate the mind on the things in the window and then later to recall as many as possible of the articles observed. A lively interest must, of course, lie back of such a practice or much of the value of it will be lost.

A promising young school teacher once said that when riding on a street car or in going to and from school, she recited to herself a new lesson in Latin or some other subject. She was the kind who would doubtless make a good school marm—but she would never be a saleswoman, unless she changed her tactics. It is actually a part of the salesman's business to be alive to the things around him so that observation becomes second nature to him. The man whose mind has been trained to observe details and to make a mental record of them quickly, will almost unconsciously store things in his mind for future reference, and an alert salesman will find no difficulty in making use of this material in interpreting human nature or in introducing a bit of conversation to take away the matter-of-factress of business. The memory of things observed is the storehouse from which the imagination draws the materials to be made into new patterns, and with these, many difficulties may be solved. There is no limit to the uses that the salesman will find for the fund of facts that he thus gathers.

AMBITION

14. A man's success depends primarily on having the right motives, on having some kind of ambition as a driving force. It is true that some have no lack of good motives, but fail to act on them; such persons, through weak wills, fail to improve themselves. Their ambitions perish at the stage when they are mere impulses or desires. Some motives or instincts are inherited. The instinct of life preservation, mother love, and other motives are well known; they lie deep in the foundation of human nature.

The man without a motive is like a rudderless ship that must sail somewhere but drifts hither and thither with no fixed direction. Many a young man has received a motive in being forced to see how much better other young men of his age are doing; or by marrying and desiring to increase his income in order to support a home; or by the desire to be well-to-do, to have luxuries, or to receive the praise of men.

A recent exhaustive study of a large force of salesmen brought to light the interesting fact that every successful man on the force had some well-defined motive or moving cause for making his work a success. In some cases, the motive was the earning of a comfortable income. In other cases, the successful salesman was a spendthrift, but lavished the money on his wife, and his satisfaction in providing her with comforts and luxuries was the motive that impelled him to exert himself.

Causes of various other kinds have been found underlying successful salesmanship—misfortune, a spirit of rivalry, love of power, etc. Practically speaking, it matters little what moves a man to activity, provided his motive is honorable. Many a man has been unaware of the great blessing that poverty has been to him in the development of his character, making it necessary for him to hustle in order to get anywhere in the world. Whatever motivates a man, whether it is duty to parents, dissatisfaction with present work, love, ambition to serve mankind better, the important thing is to have a motive that will act as a stimulus, and force one to exert himself to the utmost. A man who has a definite ambition formed will sacrifice everything else to reach his objective. He becomes aggressive and self-confident and is able to face circumstances squarely and display leadership and authority.

ENERGY

15. Need of Energy.—Ambition may well be compared to the fire under the boiler, and energy to the steam that runs the human machine. A man may have many other strong qualifications, but if he lacks energy the rich rewards of salesmanship will not be his. The person who imagines that the successful salesman has an easy time of it should not take up the work. True, he is often more independent than the office man and can manage his working hours largely to suit himself, but he must arrange his time to the best advantage if he is to make it count for success, and he must be able to back up his efforts with an energy that will overcome the indifference and sometimes the opposition of those to whom he presents his proposition.

The man who is not alert to pick up information and quick to act on it will probably be late in his dealings with firms about to place orders; and he will have a much harder fight to get business than the man who is on the ground early. Then, too, in order to have a fair chance to land a contract, a man often has to put in hard work investigating a certain situation and going well prepared. A bit of timely information may cause an enterprising salesman to take a midnight train and a long drive early the following morning in order to get an interview with his prospective customer at the right time. Sometimes, when he is thoroughly tired, it may be necessary for him to brace up and be at his best for a few hours more, in order to do justice to his employer in an important deal. At times, there may be half a dozen urgent calls to make before the departure of a train that the traveling salesman feels he should take in order to attend to important matters elsewhere. In such cases, he must be energetic in order to do his duty properly.

16. Divisions of Energy.—For convenience, energy may be divided into initiative, concentration, and persistence.

Initiative, which may be defined as the ability to start something, grows out of memory and a healthy imagination. The accident-insurance man with initiative sees in an accident in a large shop, to a man that carried a policy, a convincing example of the value of his insurance that will help him sell dozens of policies to the workers of that shop. Initiative makes him act quickly while the example is fresh in the minds of the men, and it is easy to induce them to secure policies for their own protection.

The giving of thorough attention to the work at hand is concentration, which is intense work. The accident-insurance man just referred to, if he is a good concentrator, will leave no stone unturned in his canvass of the men of the shop. Armed with a letter of gratitude from the beneficiary of the policy covering the accident, he will seek the permission of the superintendent or foreman to distribute accident-policy literature throughout the shop. He will interview all the men, knowing that sometimes the man with whom the salesman least expects to do business is the one who gives an order. The concentrative salesman will then go over the ground again and get as much business, after the field would seem to some salesmen as worked out, as he did in the first covering. The concentrator is an enthusiast, and he finds that his work develops him as well as his business. No salesman ever put through a concentrated effort without coming out a bigger man.

Thomas A. Edison's chief characteristic is the power of concentration or application. A great inventor must possess this quality to a high degree, since the attention that it creates insures a comprehensive observation of all essential details. Invention, customer analysis, analysis of goods, all depend first on attention. It is necessary to see a thing before the thing can be reasoned about; and seeing it depends on the ability to bring impressions from the outside world and stamp them upon the brain. Edison can rivet his attention upon a scientific problem for days at a time, because of his unusual power of application. A salesman that can apply himself assiduously day after day to his work shows that this one mental trait of attention is strongly developed.

Because sales managers recognize this ability to be fundamental in the success of a salesman, they seek to discover it in every applicant. If a salesman studies his proposition thoroughly, and rivets his attention upon it, he gets credit for great power of application. If he keeps after business and lands orders from a goodly proportion of his prospects, he is ranked high because of his persistence. These two expressions then, power of application and persistence, are simply different ways of describing two methods of doing hard work. Edison says that genius is the power to stick to a thing, and put hard work on it until it is done.

17. The final element of energy is persistence. When a man has thought out an idea and has worked at it with all the power he possesses, the only remaining thing needed is the persistence to keep at the job until it is finished. Thousands of good sales plans have been put down as failures because they were abandoned too soon, because the salesman lacked the ability to stick to his task until it was finished. Of course it is good judgment to abandon any plan as soon as it seems certain to be a failure and merely a waste of valuable time. But a little experimenting does not necessarily prove failure. It is a human weakness to form judgment too quickly. There are too many men who can work with great enthusiasm as long as everything goes well, but when anything apparently is wrong they cannot stick with bulldog tenacity and try plans out to the end.

"Keeping everlastingly at it brings success," is the motto of a successful selling organization. Almost any sales manager can cite cases where men of apparently no brilliancy make fine records regularly simply because of their tenacity. They go back repeatedly to see a prospect whom most men would give up after the first unsuccessful attempt. They probe persistently to the bottom of excuses and get light as to how to canvass a difficult prospect when other men would leave in disgust. Hugh Chalmers tells of an instance in his own experience where the most persistent work on a prospect seemingly failed to accomplish anything. Finally, when asked, as a favor to the salesman, to tell why he would not buy the cash register, the prospect said that he had an old employe, named Henry, who he thought would be offended if he bought the register. Getting permission to talk to Henry, the salesman soon convinced him of the value of the register, and was rewarded for his persistency by a sale.

The salesman must use judgment with his persistence. There are times when it is poor business to keep after a man, when it is good tactics to leave him, going back when circumstances are more favorable. But the salesman starting out must learn that he cannot afford to let go every time he is told that there is no business to be had; it is the natural thing to say *no* to the salesman, for people whom salesmen interview are usually on the defensive. *No* is often said when the one who says it has no knowledge of what the salesman is offering. Only by intelligent persistence can the salesman hope to overcome all the numerous excuses offered by prospects and win a chance to secure a hearing.

A successful architect in a prosperous city of the Middle West says that he was induced to raise his standard of life and acquire the ability to sell his services to infinitely better advantage through the persistence of a salesman. He says: "I was a stonecutter, earning $1.75 a day chipping marble, when the representative of a correspondence school told me of the opportunities within my grasp, provided I would study with his school. When I told him I had no time to spend in study, he said I had. When I told him I had no ability, he said I had.

I then told him I had no money to purchase such a course as he recommended; he said I had. Induced to enroll for a course by the stirring persuasion and enthusiastic arguments of the representative, I made my start and I came up—developed from a stonecutter into an architect—simply because I was led by his persistence to use the power that was latent within me."

As an example of what tactful persistence will accomplish, a house-to-house salesman of aluminum ware relates the following experience: "One day I approached a residence that had a sign on the front step, 'No peddlers or agents allowed.' I paid no attention to the sign, but rang the doorbell. When the lady of the house came to the door she was very indignant and immediately asked if I had not seen the sign on the step. I said I had, but thought she would feel very bad if I did not give her a chance to see the new line of goods I was introducing in the city. Curiosity got the better of her, and she wanted to know what I had. I told her I was showing the best line of aluminum cooking utensils on the market and asked her if she had ever used this ware. She said she had used a few small articles, but that aluminum ware was too expensive and that anyway she could get it from her husband's hardware store, for he handled aluminum ware.

"I replied, 'You are very fortunate in having such an advantage, but you cannot purchase our combination sets at any store in this city because our company does not sell them to retailers. How do you like the aluminum utensils you have used?'

"She said they were nice, but that they cost too much and that she had many pans and kettles of enamel ware that she never used and they took up valuable space in her pantry. I said, 'Yes, there is nothing more displeasing to a woman than to have a lot of things that are of little use and that take up so much room. That is exactly why so many housekeepers are buying our utensils. They are so neatly combined that you have many utensils in a compact form and they are very light, strong, and durable. I am sure you would enjoy looking at them. I am not asking that you purchase but I am advertising the utensils, and I should like to show you my samples, even if you do not purchase.' Though she said it would be a waste of time, she permitted me to show my goods, and as a result I sold her an order amounting to nearly $15.' "

These are typical instances of sales made by earnest persistence on the part of the salesman. Many new salesmen have been chagrined to find that after they had given a prospect up as hopeless, other salesmen have come along and done business with the same individual. The truth is that in many such cases the first salesman made some progress but did not hold on long enough to reap the result of his efforts, leaving his work behind to help some one else. A common illustration will make this clearer. A man goes out on the street where newsboys are numerous. Holding the paper before the man's face, a newsboy shouts "Paper, Sir"; but the man shakes his head and passes on. But, by the time several boys have solicited the prospective purchaser, some calling out the headline of the day's biggest news event or showing a front-page illustration, the man concludes that he does want a paper and he buys.

A salesman who has made wonderful records says that he spurs his energy by figuring out that the first 12 days of the month are expense days, that it takes that long to sell enough to pay his expenses, and that the remaining days of the month are profit days. He labors hard to keep the expense days from stealing any of the profit days' effort, and then when the profit days begin he works with even greater zeal, for every sale made means money in his pocket.

SELF-CONFIDENCE

18. Many men suffer from timidity and self-consciousness. One of the best-known salesmen in New York City says that when he first left an inside job to take up selling work he sometimes walked up and down in front of a place of business, hesitating to go inside to ask for an order, even when he had good reason to believe that the order could be had. But by the right sort of mental discipline he overcame the weakness and for years has enjoyed unusual success. To see that man today one would never imagine that he suffered at one time from timidity.

Doctor O. S. Marden says: "Timidity, shyness, and self-consciousness belong to the same family. We usually find all where we find one, and they are all enemies of peace of mind, happiness, and achievement. No one has ever done a great thing while his mind was centered upon himself. We must lose ourselves before we can find ourselves. Self-analysis is valuable only to learn our strength; it is fatal if it makes us dwell upon our weakness."

The timid man exaggerates every slight or failure. He seems to be looking for something to make him realize his own weakness. Things that other people would take no notice of or pass with a smile, he takes much to heart, and loses valuable time in revolving them over in his mind. There is no need to go into further details of this weakness, for it is common enough to be known by all. The best remedy is to plunge right into work and mix with people, some of whom will have little regard for a man's timidity. The handling he will get will give him the best lessons he ever learned. He should dress well, for the knowledge that he has a good appearance goes far toward dispelling timidity. He should give himself stern lectures. He should say as one young man did: "Now, Arthur, either there is something in you or there is not; and I am going to find out. Do not be a fool. You are just as good as anybody else, so long as you behave well. Hold up your head and be a man. Do not be afraid to face anybody. Go about among people as though you were somebody. Quit this everlasting self-depreciation, self-effacement. You have just as good a right on this glad green earth as anybody else."

One sales manager says to timid men that he employs: "Throw your shoulders back and walk up to every man as if he owed you ten dollars." When the timid man has dealt with a few dozens of men he is not long in finding out that a man is nothing but a man, no matter if he is president of a big corporation, and that the man-fear is nothing but a delusion. The gruffest men have good qualities when they are known well.

After all, every man knows it is silly, even laughable, to have fear of other men, when all that one may do to a salesman who bears himself courteously is to be inconsiderate, discourteous, or insulting, and that always harms the man guilty of such action more than it does any one else. The timid, sensitive man is usually gifted with a fine nature that counts for much when some of his tender spots have become hardened by constant contact with the busy world.

Knowledge, courage, and confidence go hand in hand; to some extent they overlap. A man knowing thoroughly a certain line of business is likely to believe in himself. He would be a rare man who could have knowledge and courage without self-reliance. The successful salesman needs to understand not only himself but the business he represents. If he lacks confidence, he should study the business and get this quality or else give up the vocation, for nothing is more certain than that a man cannot do his best work in a calling that does not command the best in him.

A man cannot have thorough belief in himself without having something substantial on which to base his faith. Belief without a fundamental element of available fact is a delusion; it amounts to a bluff, which does not stand in these days of keen competition and commercial publicity. Specific knowledge of his business and of himself is the corner stone of self-confidence. The glib talker is at a disadvantage in competition with a salesman of superior equipment. Ordinarily, it is the amount and quality of accessible, specific information a salesman has that tends to establish self-confidence and to give him the requisite courage to stand before a prospective customer and deliver a convincing talk on the desirability of his goods.

Specific knowledge steadies the surgeon's hand and gives him courage to perform an operation where a life is at stake. To acquire similar confidence, the salesman should get in touch with the most successful salesmen his house has on the road, learn what they know and how they apply their knowledge.

Confidence in self is increased by each victory and by a philosophical view of all failures. Few attempts, when a man has done his best, can, with strict accuracy, be called failures. Each is a profitable experience. The man who has faith in himself and the business he represents knows that his inability to carry his point occasionally is merely an incident. He knows that he has the power that must eventually pull him through. So he merely looks to details to see what is wrong when the order fails to come, but optimistically perseveres.

<hr />

ENTHUSIASM

19. Enthusiasm grows out of knowledge and confidence. The enthusiastic man knows, and is confident that he knows. He finds joy in telling others about his subject. His eyes and his manner convey almost as much of his message as what he puts into words. Love for one's work may be said to be contagious. It seems to be in the air when the enthusiastic man is before his customer, and the customer's mind responds in spite of himself; the calm objections that he may have held in reserve for the salesman's argument sometimes vanish without utterance before the pervading influence of enthusiasm. The purchaser feels that the other man is so full of his subject and so sure of his knowledge that he must be right.

Enthusiasm gives the salesman that slight mental advantage which is so important at the very outset of negotiations. The salesman who, in an indifferent state of mind, approaches a prospect, is likely to lose the sale unless the demand is strong enough to bring the sale through despite the lack of force in the salesman's attitude. "Have you any card-filing cases?" asked a customer in a stationery store. "Indeed we have—a fine assortment," replied the salesman. His first sentence contained only six words, but they stood for sixty. They proved that the stock of cases was one that he was thoroughly familiar with, one that he took pride in showing and that he could show well. He had his sale well started when he had uttered his six-word sentence of enthusiasm.

Enthusiasm not only swells the sales total but makes selling a pleasure. It overrides the obstacles that the unenthusiastic salesman finds formidable and brings him to the close of his day with a feeling that work is a great blessing and the ability to take his evening meal with the assurance that the day has been well spent.

The way to possess enthusiasm is for a salesman to get a full knowledge of himself and the goods he has to sell. A person who is full of zeal and fervor imparts his earnestness to others. An inspired sales manager will often make his men enthusiastic by his attitude and expressions. Therefore, it is a good plan for a salesman to get in touch with ardent people in the same line of work. Such contact is often the making of a man who has felt himself weak and discouraged.

OPTIMISM

20. The trait that enables men to look on the bright side of things, to hope for and believe in the best, is termed optimism; pessimism is the opposite trait, that which makes men look on the dark side. Some one has given the humorous illustration that the optimist sees the doughnut, while the pessimist gazes on nothing but the hole. Optimism is an important trait for the salesman. He cannot expect to make a success of every attempt at a sale, so he not only needs the ability to look on apparent failures philosophically but to regard them as distinct gains in experience, though as far as immediate sales results are concerned, they may be fruitless.

Then, too, optimism is greatly to be desired for its effect on the customer. Every one feels better for contact with a man who has faith in the future, whose face beams with good cheer. The pessimist is depressing. Most people have enough gloom in their own lives to fight away, and they have no time, in business hours, for the grouch, complainer, or calamity prophet. Panics are brought about by pessimism. One man talks about them to another, the second informs a third, and soon the mischief is done. Normal conditions are not restored until the optimists begin to say: "Here, what's the matter? Everything is all right; of course it is, and it's going to keep on being right." The customer who may be discouraged over something in his own business is helped by the aggressive, optimistic man who comes in as a ray of sunshine, whose very presence is a support, a tonic.

It is undeniable that some men are born with happier, more philosophical dispositions than others, but it is also true that pessimism and worry are evil habits that fasten themselves like parasites on the mind and rob it of its powers and the joy of living. The optimists have their hours of trial; they come through experiences chastened but with more power for the days ahead. Every man who has had long periods of pessimism and worry can look back afterwards, smile, and see how he allowed himself to distort the facts; that, after all, there was no occasion for gloom. An old man on his deathbed, said to his sons, "Boys, I have had a lot of trouble, but most of it never happened."

The cure for pessimism is to give oneself strong suggestions of optimism. If the victory cannot be won alone, recourse may be had to some optimistic acquaintance who will chase away the ghosts of doubt and fear. Of late years, much has been written about the Emanuel Movement and similar efforts of well-meaning men to help along those whose mental and moral health need attention. Their method is to look carefully into the source of weakness and then to give suggestions that sink deep into the subject's mind and enable him to overcome the trouble. There is nothing new in the principle that these men, interested in the well-being of their fellows, are using. They are merely doing in an organized way what has been done haphazardly for many years, and they are doing their work more effectively because they have made a better study of the mind than their predecessors. No doubt every man can recall instances when he was greatly strengthened by the words of a person of strong character, who went into the details of some cause of worry, showed how little there was to worry about, allayed the fears, and made the way out of the situation clear. But valuable as counsel and suggestions from others sometimes are, there is no need for seeking such aid continually. Man has latent powers that he needs but to call forth in order to win most of his victories. When his appeal goes out for extra power, and he has faith to believe that he can have it, he has but to proceed along rational lines in order to win a victory.

No matter what tide of pessimism and discouragement may sometimes sweep over a man, he should tell himself that all is not lost, and that all will be well in due time. Often all that is needed in such a case is a little relaxation, a change of scene, a drive, a good laugh, or something else that will rest the mind and permit it to take the normal view of things. Many men have been saved from dangerous pessimism by taking a little vacation or by participating in some game in which they had to exercise their muscles, but gave rest to some overworked brain cells.

COURTESY

21. One of the greatest assets that a salesman can have is courtesy. A salesman who is considerate of others is able to gain his point in many cases where all other tactics would fail. The president of the great Chemical Bank of New York says: "If I could speak twenty languages, I would preach courtesy in them all."

It should be remembered that courtesy is more than mere politeness. Politeness, which is only the outward expression of courtesy, includes such acts as removing the hat in the presence of women, giving deference to elderly people, saying "I thank you," and other expressions that show good manners and good breeding. In addition to these niceties of conduct, courtesy includes a more important point—a sincere consideration of the rights and feelings of others. While acts of politeness are necessary, the truly successful salesmen attribute their success to courtesy in the broadest sense of the word —the ability to consider the viewpoint of prospects and make the transaction profitable to them.

Once the salesman realizes the importance of courtesy, he will leave nothing undone to develop the quality to the highest degree possible. If he is in doubt as to whether he is as courteous as he should be, he should ask some one who has a chance to observe him, and who can be depended on for a frank opinion. Associating with well-bred people is one good way of training himself in this quality, but courtesy can be developed fully only by using as his guide the golden rule of doing unto others as he would have them to do unto him.

---

22. What Tact Includes.—Tact is that quality in a salesman which enables him to adapt his words, manners, and actions so as to be agreeable to those with whom he comes into contact. It implies patience, cheerfulness, gracious acceptance of an inevitable situation, the ability to understand others and to be broad-minded and generous in considering them and their faults, and the power of quick decision as to the best thing to do or to say.

A tactful salesman does not smoke in the presence of a buyer unless he is sure that doing so will not give offense. He keeps his. temper when opposition is unavoidable and keeps himself under control. A tactful salesman knows that once a prospective buyer is offended the possibilities for making a sale are greatly lessened. He does not discuss politics or religion unless he is sure that his views on either of these subjects are agreeable to the person with whom he is conversing. He is extremely careful about criticising competitors. When a salesman enters an office, takes up the goods of a competitor which may be lying around, and starts to point out defects and errors, he may be reflecting on the good judgment of the man he is addressing. Possibly the thing he is condemning was bought from his rival after careful deliberation by the purchaser, and to be abruptly shown that it was a mistake to buy is not pleasing to the customer, to say the least.

A salesman's tact is put to a most trying test when catering to the egotism of some business men. Flattery is disgusting, and a fine distinction must be drawn between catering to a man's egotism, and mere flattery. The knack of doing the former, of giving the egotist due credit for what he is without piling up praise, being deferential without fawning and submerging one's own convictions, will give a man a willing ear and the respect of those with whom he does business.

K S F—5

23. Examples of the Value of Tact.—A very successful traveling salesman always removed his hat just as he greeted his prospective customer; the manner in which he did this made a favorable impression, and gave the salesman an opportunity to introduce his business in an effective way. This is an example of tactful action; and it should be understood that tact in manner and action is often of just as great importance as tact in words.

A woman went shopping for a hat, taking a friend with her. While she was trying on a hat that she liked very well, her friend offered an opinion without being asked, saying, "Of course, red is awfully stylish, but you know *you* can't wear it, with your face as red as a beet." The well-trained saleswoman, realizing that this remark had put the prospect in an unreceptive frame of mind, said, "Madam's cheeks are like roses; she can afford to wear many of these quieter tones that most women feel they must avoid."

The value of tact is illustrated in the case of two salesmen. One, who is uniformly courteous, invited a customer who did not buy, although he had taken considerable time to examine certain articles, to call again and thanked him for his consideration and attention. To all outward appearances he showed as much appreciation as if a large order had been given.

He made a good impression on the customer and established good-will. The other salesman, in his anxiety to display his brilliant accomplishments, constantly interrupted the prospect on whom he was calling. He became ruffled and impetuous. He was irritable when the least criticism was offered. When he failed to secure an order he showed plainly that he was disappointed. This man left without showing the slightest appreciation for the time given him. The man addressed was made to feel that he would not care to see that salesman again.

A magazine solicitor once went into the office of an advertising agency, and, talking to the man who had made up the list of publications for the advertising of a home fire-extinguisher, spoke contemptuously of certain magazines included. Declaring them to be cheap trash, he said, "Why not use a magazine like mine, when practically every subscriber we have owns a home?" He had an excellent argument, but his ill-spirited criticism of the agency man's judgment did no good. The agency man, with good self-control, referred with a little touch of humor to the other man's righteous indignation, but he did not change his list. If, in this case, the solicitor had concealed his ill will and proceeded in an earnest, forceful way to show the agency man how the list of publications could be improved, he would likely have gained his point.

A newspaper solicitor whose paper was already carrying small single-column advertisements of a savings bank, noticed that the same institution was running a series of double-column advertisements in a rival paper. Rushing to see the man who controlled the advertising, who was, by the way, a man of considerable experience in financial publicity, he said, with a familiarity that was out of place with the man he was talking to, "Say, old man, why can't we have that big copy you are running with the ———?" This was a poor way to begin his argument for the bigger copy, and he proceeded to be still less tactful by turning over the pages of his paper, referring to the space of the bank as "dinky," and comparing it with the advertisements that other banks were displaying in the newspaper. When he went further and began, with much positiveness, to tell the advertising man that quadrupling the space would give about eight times as much force, the latter began to grow sarcastic and asked if a half page would not be better, if a full page would not be still better, if two full pages would not pay still more proportionately, and finally ran the solicitor's argument out to absurdity. The interview wound up in a controversy. As a result the solicitor afterwards had a hard time to do business with that bank's advertising man. His lack of tact proved costly.

SELF-CONTROL

24. Need of Self-Control.—The salesman should always have himself absolutely under control; the person who cannot control himself cannot hope to succeed in leading and controlling others.

The salesman will meet people who are unpleasant to deal with. But it does no good, when dealing with people who are disagreeable, to lose one's temper and speak sharply. It is often advisable for a man to preserve his self-respect, but this should be done in a dignified, manly way rather than by descending to the methods of the street brawler.

A national advertiser who was constantly in a state of partial intoxication once endeavored to insult a newspaper solicitor by declaring that he did not know him, had never advertised in his paper, though the solicitor had called to renew a contract that expired the following week. He wound up by asking why the solicitor came around bothering him, declaring that he didn't want to be annoyed but would do business with the paper direct if he ever wanted to advertise in its columns, and so on. The solicitor heard him through, merely looking his man straight in the eye, and keeping back hot replies. Finally, when the advertiser had ceased his ire-arousing talk, the solicitor asked, "Have you finished?" He then went on firmly, stepping inside the little office gate to show the big man that he was not in the least intimidated: "I have come down here on a business errand. You don't have to do business with my paper unless you want to; we don't have to carry your advertising; we can get along without it; but you will have to talk to me like a business man." He spoke without anger, but with considerable firmness, and he forced the other man to discuss the renewal in a businesslike way. This solicitor secured not only a renewal but an apology, and he went off feeling that he had won a victory, whereas a sensitive, hot-tempered man would merely have raised a general row and accomplished nothing.

Every one will concede the value of self-control. The question is how to control the emotions. It is natural, when insulted, to lose one's temper, and to pay the other man back in like manner. The fact is that some men purposely make temper-trying remarks to embarrass salesmen. When the latter yields to the temptation he is falling into the trap and furnishing the other man a good excuse for terminating the interview. There is an old rule about counting ten before speaking, in times when it is difficult to control the feelings. It was founded on a good principle, that of giving reason a chance to control the natural emotions. Modern psychologists advise a man, under trying circumstances, to suggest to himself: "Look out now; here is trouble. Go slow. Don't fall all over yourself and make a mess of it. A little careful handling will do for this fellow." This advice is easier to give than to carry out, but the man who controls himself once has started the habit of self-control and thereafter finds it easier to hold the reins on himself. Self-control relates not merely to the temper but to every other weakness: loose or profane talking, idling, drinking, immorality, discouragement, etc.

25. How to Develop Self-Control.—Man never becomes a perfect master of his emotions. He cannot make himself proof against the natural impulses that now and then surge up. He is human and cannot make himself an unfeeling machine. But his wonderful mental make-up does not leave him without the means to check and largely control the emotions. There are several things that can be done in controlling the emotions:

1. The powers of reason control the muscles and can refuse to let them act. A man, when highly insulted, cannot check the increase in heart beats or the rush of blood to the head that such excitement causes, but anger cannot rise to a high pitch until the jaws are shut down, the hands clenched, or other physical manifestations take place. By using the reason to check these accompaniments of anger, by keeping the hands open and forcing a smile, an effective curb is provided.

2. Reason also has the power to restrain the body from such environment as is likely to excite the emotions. The man whose weakness is liquor knows well enough that it is easier to avoid drinking places than it is to resist temptation when the smell of intoxicants is under his nose. Reason, too, when one has inadvertently been put in an environment likely to arouse harmful emotions, prompts the muscles to act in getting out of the danger zone: "This is a bad situation for you," warns the inner voice, "better get out of it right away before you are caught."

3. Reason has the power to call on the imagination and picture the dark side of the result if dangerous emotions are yielded to, and thus offsets the attractions or force of the emotions. When the temptation is strong toward doing nothing, the imagination can quickly sketch the result of the idleness and how that conclusion compares with the effect of industry. If tempted to dissipation, the imagination readily pictures the physical exhaustion, time wasted, loss of self-respect, etc., that debauchery always brings and which every man knows overbalance any fleeting satisfaction that the yielding to temptation has afforded.

As the harmful emotions are held in check, the pictures they create gradually become less vivid. If they are not combatted, the pictures become more and more vivid. It is a law of memory that those things which are not recalled fade away gradually. Therefore, every victory over unworthy impulses weakens the power of the emotions and correspondingly strengthens their guardian. Every man should be always ready with his autosuggestions and fight hard for victory over every impulse that tends to rob him of any of the strong, noble manhood that is his heritage.

JUDGMENT

26. Judgment grows out of experience. No man can judge perfectly, but some men, by broad experience and rational thinking, acquire a degree of good judgment that distinguishes them from their fellows. It is sometimes said that judgment cannot be learned, but this is not true. A sales manager may give a man a problem, then show him the errors he made in solving it and explain the right way to handle it. In this way, the man is taught how to deal with that class of problems, and the knowledge he acquires on various classes of problems makes his reasoning more accurate and his general judgment better. But it is not always necessary for him to solve a problem or make a mistake in order to gain in judgment; he should learn from the experience of others, although some things do not seem to pass into judgment until each man has passed through the experience for himself. Older persons usually have better judgment than younger persons. They have passed through more experiences and their own mistakes and successes, and their observation of the mistakes and successes of others, have given them better reasoning powers.

The man of good judgment must be a clear thinker. To develop this quality, a man should accustom himself to look thoroughly into problems before acting, or at least to look into them as thoroughly as time permits. He should invariably consider all the phases of a situation before doing anything. Then, having thoroughly investigated and carefully formed his conclusions, he should have enough confidence in himself to stand by his judgments unless developments show clearly that he is mistaken. The man who cannot make up his mind or who flits nervously from one decision to another is unfortunate. His fears that he may have decided wrong leave him abstracted and unfit to give attention to his work. It is better to drive away determinedly, even if a mistake is made occasionally, than to be forever faltering and looking back. The man who cannot make up his mind and stick to his decisions is handicapped and never has a chance to show his true worth.

Mistakes are regrettable, but they usually leave a consolation prize in the shape of experience that increases judgment. That salesman had the right spirit who, after losing a chance to secure an order, said, "I see why I lost, but next time I'll know just how to do it," and who later went back to that same prospect and made a sale.

———

INTEGRITY

27. Essential in a Well-Rounded Personality.—Integrity is a characteristic that embodies moral soundness and freedom from dishonest practices of every sort. It is, therefore, a quality that is essential to the development of a complete and well-rounded personality. There is no lasting success possible in business for a man who is unscrupulous, but lack of integrity is especially fatal in selling work. A salesman is peculiarly liable to temptations, and the development of dishonest habits is easy.

This quality is of much greater importance to the salesman, and to the employer of salesmen than one might be inclined to think without analyzing it thoroughly. Employers generally think of integrity largely as it applies to honesty in money matters. But there are several other aspects of integrity that the salesman should consider. It is often said that time is an important element in the salesman's success; that is, the salesman who knows how to employ his time to the best advantage succeeds more readily than does the one who squanders his time. But the salesman should thoroughly understand that the man who squanders or misuses his employer's time knowingly is dishonest in that respect—he lacks integrity to that extent. Likewise the salesman who knowingly renders a false report to his firm is dishonest—he cheats his employer just as much as if he were to take money deliberately from the cash drawer. The salesman who makes false excuses for his negligence, the salesman who fails to safeguard his employer's business, the salesman who does not cooperate to the best of his ability with other employes cannot be said to possess real sterling integrity.

28. Some Types That Lack Integrity.—The advantages possessed by a man of a certain worthy quality sometimes stand out more prominently when he is contrasted with men of opposite qualities. The contrast here is especially valuable.

1. *The Guesser.*—This is the salesman who is likely to guess at things, particularly facts regarding his business, in order to be able to make an interesting report. The man of this type is apt to take passing remarks of customers, and even the casual remarks of disinterested persons as facts. One salesman of this type won the confidence and the admiration of his employer by making definite, though unverified, statements regarding conditions pertaining to his business. For instance, he would send in a report to his firm stating that 70 per cent. of the people in certain customer's territory ate a given amount of a certain kind of cereal, or 67 per cent. of the people wore a certain kind of garment, etc. He was regarded as a valuable employe, until it was found that he was merely guessing.

2. *The Excuse Maker.*—A manager employing a large number of salesmen remarked that he had one of the most complete weather reports in the world, outside of the regular official government reports. Then he explained that he had a large force of men covering the entire country, and their daily reports were filled with excuses blaming the weather and other external and more or less irrelevant things for their failure to produce a satisfactory amount of business.

It may seem a little thing for a salesman to offer an excuse for his failure. The excuse may be entirely sincere—it may be reasonable. But it is a dangerous thing for any one, particularly the salesman, to fall into the habit of trying to find a good excuse for every failure to produce satisfactory results. It is such a short step from the excuse to out-and-out dishonesty. Let a person find that it is possible to deceive his employer with a clever excuse and he will be very much inclined to fall into the habit of making excuses for every shortcoming, the first step in a certain kind of dishonesty. The courageous salesman will dare to face the whole world even when he meets defeat, tell the truth and take the consequences. Sometimes excuses seem little, but every little excuse is a stepping-stone to a bigger fault.

3. *The Loafer.*—The loafer and the excuse maker are closely related. It is but a step from deceiving with an excuse to deliberate neglect of duty. Loafing is dishonest, for it robs the employer of time he pays for; thus it really robs him of money. A salesman who had been extraordinarily successful in a territory where another man had barely made a living for a number of years, asked the salesmanager to what he attributed his success in that difficult territory. The salesmanager remarked, "We have other men who perhaps know much more than you know, we have some men who might be considered more handsome, we have some who are younger and more active, we have others who are older and much more experienced—but you possess one quality that comparatively few salesmen have; that is, honest industry. You never loaf, and it is the way you use your time that counts more than any other one thing."

The loafer's theory of life is to do as little as possible, and get as much as possible for it. The loafer is lazy both physically and mentally. Thinking is hard work; therefore, he does not think any more than is absolutely necessary to get through his daily routine. The loafer is the fellow who does not believe in working on Saturday, and he does not like to get into his territory before noon on Monday; he argues that customers do not like to buy goods on Saturday and do not like to entertain salesmen on Monday before things have been straightened out after the Saturday rush.

4. *The Liar.*—Another type of salesman that lacks integrity is the out-and-out dishonest person, who intentionally misrepresents facts. The liar will make false statements to his employer regarding business conditions, competition, prices, quality, etc. He will misrepresent to his customer. He may be shrewd and cunning; he may have an oily tongue, his arguments may seem logical—but he will be found out. The liar is a menace to himself, to his employer, and to his employer's customers. He finds no welcome anywhere in the modern business world; and sooner or later will find it impossible to secure a respectable position.

29. Honesty and Sincerity.—In every character that possesses integrity, honesty, and sincerity are always found developed to a marked degree. The insincere man usually betrays himself. No matter how much he may protest his interest and good-will, a lack of sincerity will be detected. The sincere salesman takes a real interest in persons with whom he deals. He serves them to the best of his ability and practices the golden rule.

The dishonest man often flourishes for a time. Sometimes it seems to the honest man who has to compete with fraudulent people that the adage "Honesty is the best policy" cannot be right. But in the end the dishonest man comes to grief of some kind. And who wants extra money if it is obtained with loss of respect, the constant fear of discovery, and an eventual evil reputation among his fellows? The honest man's force is cumulative. Sooner or later his square dealings build up a reputation that no one can take away. The careers of great merchants have shown beyond a doubt that it is not only better morals but actually better business to deal squarely with their customers. As yet the world is far from being perfect; but a comparison of the merchandising of the present with that of 50 years ago shows a great advance in honesty, open-and-above-board policy, the cutting out of graft, rebates, etc.

MEMORY HELPS

He who can answer the following questions from memory has a good understanding of the text in the preceding pages.

(1)   Define personality.

(2)   What three elements does personality include?

(3)   How can the imagination be trained?

(4)   How does observation help a salesman?

(5)   What is the value of ambition as an element of personality?

(6)   Name some motives that stimulate ambition.

(7)   Name some instances when energy is a valuable aid to the salesman.

(8)   What is initiative?

(9)   What is meant by combining judgment and persistence?

(10)   What is the basis of enthusiasm?

(11)   How can pessimism be cured?

(12)   What is the difference between politeness and courtesy?

(13)   Define as fully as possible tact.

(14)   Why does a salesman need the quality of self-control?

(15)   Can judgment be developed? How?

(16)   Name some types of men that lack integrity.

(17)   What is integrity?

MENTAL EFFICIENCY
(PART 2)

THE WILL

1. What the Will Is.—The will may be briefly defined as that force of the mind by which we compel ourselves to act in a definite, rational manner, even against our impulses and desires. The will almost defies analysis; it is the expression of the entire character in action.

Dr. Nathan Oppenheim defines will as follows: "Will is the conscious choosing of an idea or course of action out of a number of possible ideas or courses; and after the choosing has been done, a steady adherence to the thing preferred." This definition is a good one because it emphasizes the fact that the operation of the will involves conscious choice, action in accordance with that conscious choice, and, in the steady adherence to the thing preferred (provided the preference is a proper one), the formation of right habits which are sure to aid in the development of a worthy character.

2. Value of a Well-Trained Will.—Concerning the value of a well-trained will, William James, the eminent psychologist, says: "No one ever won success without great will power to eternally hold him to it, in the face of opposing difficulties. Even great abilities without it are of little use; they are not forced to leave their mark. A person of only medium talents, but of great strength of will, can, by keeping always at the one thing, win a great success."

The man who develops his will can not only force himself to do things that he should do; he can also force himself to refrain from doing things he should not do. It does not require the use of the will to do things we like to do or things that we find it easy to do, just as no motor power is required to move an automobile down hill. But the power of the will must be used if we are to do things that are difficult or distasteful to us. It is easy to talk to the customer who is interested, but it may be hard to overcome his objections. The salesman whose will power is weak will give up quickly when he meets opposition, but the salesman who has developed a strong will power will persist and patiently use every effort to overcome the prospect's resistance.

There is encouragement in the adage, "Where there's a will there's a way." The man who says, "I can do this thing because I have made up my mind to it," is the winner in every field—in war, in politics, and in business.

The salesman who faces great difficulties must feel that he can win because he has willed to do so. Great achievements are founded upon a desire to win, backed by the determination to succeed. The man of will succeeds because he forces himself to overcome great difficulties. The first step a person takes toward success in doing a thing he is qualified to do, is to believe he can do it. But that is not enough to win success against odds. He must also have the will to do —to persist, to persevere, to rise again when he stumbles and falls, to return to the attack when he seems to be defeated, to take a fresh hold when things seem to be slipping from his grasp.

One of the great stores of Chicago is owned and conducted by brothers who tramped the dusty country roads throughout the middle west for years, carrying packs, endeavoring to get together enough money to start a little store in the city. Today as the great throngs pass through the magnificently equipped establishment one often hears the remark that one can accomplish great things if he only has the capital to start with, but people do not realize that all the capital these men had to start with was contained within their own minds—it was the will to achieve a definite object. Their original capital was not in gold, but it was of even greater value. It was not acceptable as legal tender, but it succeeded where money has often failed.

The study of the career of almost any great captain of industry reveals the fact that in addition to ability he has had a strong will. The will to do coupled with moderate ability is stronger than great capacity plus a weak will.

3. Will Power Can Be Developed.—Some persons are born with stronger wills than others, as some are born with stronger muscles. But the will can be developed and strengthened. If one's will is not strong one must exercise it so that it will grow in strength. Emerson said, "Anyone with an ordinary brain can make good if he has the willingness to run that brain to, say, 80 per cent. of its highest efficiency." Developing the will increases one's power for success.

One should not make the mistake of confusing will power and stubbornness—many people who boast of their will power are only stubborn or obstinate. Sheer obstinacy is a misuse of the will in persisting in error. The will should be trained to serve good and useful ends; to persist in error is useless and harmful. A man should harness his will and direct it as a force that will enable him to carry into effect those things which will help himself and others.

As the will must take account of the emotions, there can be no such thing as training the will as if it were a separate organ, an arm, or a leg. Education of the will means education of the impulses. The men at the top are subject to the same feelings as others, but they stand out as leaders because they have the will power to control and suppress their impulses. They have learned that the man who would control others must first master himself. All true education may be called will training. Every decision well thought out, made resolutely, and adhered to firmly, trains the will for better work. Likewise, careless, hasty thinking, the habit of acting solely on impulse, of vacillating from one judgment to another before being convinced of error, of having few self-formed opinions and indulging the habit of relying largely on others, tend to retard the development of will power.

A man can develop his will power by constantly doing what he believes to be the right and proper thing, even in very small matters, and by steadfastly refusing to make compromises when such compromises are clearly wrong. Most men's characters are affected infinitely more by the little things than by the great things. Through obstinacy or neglect, their wills fail to act on little duties that the inner voice whispers should be faced cheerfully. And these things are not always the ones that the world sees. The building up of the character is determined largely by the decisions within oneself on matters that others may know nothing of—decisions that are made, not for other men's praise or favor, but because they seem right.

4. Elements of Will Power.—Perhaps one reason why so many persons fail to develop the will is that they do not realize, first of all, that will power is made up of a number of well-defined elements, each plainly recognizable in itself, and that each of these must be developed to bring the will power up to a desirable standard. The person who has the right kind of will power—the kind that brings success in a worthy aim—possesses, either by natural gift or by development, the following elemental qualities: definiteness, prompt decision, self-confidence, self-control, and persistence.

Definiteness.—The person endeavoring to develop the will should mark well the principle—*first will to do, and then do.* He should know what he is about. He must determine to act—then act. When he knows he should do a thing he should say to himself, *There is but one way—that way is to do this thing.* All the fine resolution in the world will avail nothing unless one forces oneself to positive action.

Every action should be made to count. Things must be done with a purpose. Thought must precede action, then the action must be performed promptly in a definite and positive manner; there must be no hesitation, worry, or drifting with the current.

There is a definite connection between desire and will. The more intense one's desire is for anything, the greater will be the will power exerted to secure that thing. A person may want something but may lack the will power to make the effort necessary to get it.

In order to crystallize desire into will it is necessary to intensify the desire until it irresistibly drives the will to make the necessary effort. The best way to stimulate a desire so that desire is crystallized into will is to dwell persistently upon the advantages of that which is desired. This will invariably arouse a sluggish will to action.

Prompt Decision.—Prompt decision is a distinguishing mark of the leader. The person who wavers and hesitates, who cannot reach a quick decision after he has had an opportunity to consider a proposition, is lacking in an important quality of leadership. Indecision characterizes people who follow. The successful man must be a man of decision. The salesman is called upon many times each day to decide quickly what he should do in the conduct of a sales interview. Persons of strong will power make up their minds far more readily than do those whose wills are weak. Of course, the ability to decide correctly comes with experience. Yet there are many people of wide experience who for lack of will power seem unable to decide matters. They find themselves depending on others for help and suggestions. There are men who will take a long time to decide whether they will buy a pair of white suspenders or blue ones.

To get the habit of making prompt decisions, a person must simply consider the alternatives involved, concentrate his thought on the business in hand, and draw upon his experience, but when the evidence is all in, he must decide and act.

Some men can accomplish so much in a day because they have learned to act quickly and think quickly. A man can train his mind to act quickly just as easily as he can learn to walk fast. He can saunter down the street, taking half an hour to walk a mile, or he can speed up and walk two miles in the same time. Likewise, he can sit and worry and use an hour in deciding to do a trivial thing, or he can force himself to do the same thing in a few minutes.

K S F—6

One must be careful, however, to distinguish between prompt decisions based on a thoughtful weighing of the evidence, and impulsive conclusions. Many people act quickly, but through impulse alone, and those who are guided only by their impulses are likely to make many mistakes. The average man who follows his impulse to speculate is not as likely to make a permanent financial success as is the average man who weighs carefully each investment proposition that is presented to him. To be sure, he must have had experience in order to weigh the evidence intelligently. But he must also be able to reach prompt decisions or the best opportunities will escape him.

Self-Confidence.—Trying to develop will power without self-confidence is like trying to sail a boat without a breeze to fill the sail; we can not accomplish much so long as we feel that we have not the ability to do it. Many men have been defeated because they believed they could not succeed. When a person thinks, and feels that others think, that he can do no more than ordinary things, it becomes next to impossible for him to succeed in any great undertaking; he lacks the self-confidence without which little can be accomplished.

Self-confidence is not egotism. Self-confidence is belief in one's ability to succeed. Egotism is vanity. People admire self-confidence, especially if they can see that one's self-confidence is well-founded; but the vain, or egotistical, individual is heartily disliked. Persons who lack confidence in their own ability are greatly handicapped and should cultivate a positive mental attitude. Confidence should radiate from every action, every movement, and every word in meeting people. It is contagious and if a person acts as though he knew his business, others will think that he does know it, and in time he will develop the mental attitude of faith in himself.

Self-Control.—Self-control is one of the most important of the elements of will power. Self-control, through the use of will power, enables one to give up habits that weaken the sales personality, whether these habits are physical, as the eating of too much rich food, trying to get along with too little sleep, etc.; or mental, as worrying, reaching hasty conclusions, and indulging in pessimism.

Many things happen daily to disturb the equilibrium of the salesman. Some customers are discourteous, some are unreasonable, many of them complain without just cause. If he loses his self-control, he will lose sales, lose customers, make himself less valuable to the firm, and may even lose his job. The salesman who has the will power to restrain his impulse to retaliate when a customer is impolite or unreasonable has a great advantage over his weaker associate who gets into an argument, and thereby antagonizes the customer. By exercising self-control through the will, one may find an opportunity to change the customer's attitude to one of friendliness and appreciation.

Detailed suggestions for the development of self-control were given in *Mental Efficiency,* Part 1.

Persistence.—The will can be greatly strengthened by forcing one's self to do persistently things that require an effort. It should become a practice to use the will power constantly —to compel oneself to do promptly and thoroughly the things that should be done, and to be patient and persevering. To do the things one enjoys doing or things one is obliged to do, such as arriving at the office at 9 o'clock under penalty of a reprimand or worse, if one is late, does not require much will power. But it may be a severe test for some salesmen, when they are left to their own initiative, to call on prospects 6 hours a day.

In developing will power, persistence should be combined with concentration. For example, it is a good practice to sit perfectly still for 5 minutes, thinking persistently of some problem to be solved, such as a good answer to a hard objection that is frequently raised by prospects. Then the time may be increased to 10 or 15 minutes, the mind being kept focused on the problem, not allowed to wander. Gradually one can build up the habit of concentrated attention.

5. Some Things to Avoid.—In developing will power there are some definite things to be avoided because they are fundamentally negative and have a tendency to weaken the will. Very often it is found that the real cause of failure lies in some of the negative qualities that have prevented the development of strong will power in the individual.

Worry.—Worry is one of the worst enemies of will power. A man cannot develop his will power when he allows himself to be dominated by worry. The person who is inclined to worry should remember that worry is largely a fear of things that may never happen and a state of uneasiness over things that are past and beyond help. One imagines that something *MAY* happen that he does not wish to happen. Such imaginings are often so powerful in their effect as to cause the individual to become ill.

The salesman who makes some blunder or fails in something he had hoped to achieve, allows the memory of his failure to disturb his mind. The result of such worries over things that have gone wrong or over imagined happenings of the future is a depressed state of mind that may become morbid. Thousands of salesmen have worried themselves into complete failure. Worry is cowardice. Brave people don't worry. Pessimists worry; optimists do not. Worry can be defeated by the will. There should be a determination to harbor positive thoughts of success and happiness. If a man finds himself beginning to worry over something, he should summon his will power to make him think pleasant, happy thoughts. There is a good old adage, "Don't worry about anything you can't help, and don't worry about anything you can help." Live up to this adage and you will be happier and more successful.

Nervousness.—There are many people who are nervous through habit. This is a bad habit. It makes concentration of mind more difficult. A person can break himself of such nervous habits as fidgeting, toying with a pencil, drumming on the desk with his fingers, only by exercising his will power. He can force himself to sit still and to think.

Annoyance.—One should always avoid the expression of annoyance. Especially should one refrain from showing annoyance over petty things. The salesman may find another ahead of him calling upon his customer; but he weakens himself if he permits himself to be annoyed or to give expression to his annoyance, if he feels it. He should remain undisturbed, not only in order that others may not observe that he is annoyed, but in order that he may feel calm and be master of himself. In such a state of mind he will not be weakened when he approaches the next customer.

Anger.—There are persons who can not play a game without becoming angry when something happens that is not as they think it should be. Anger is a strong emotion and tends to overthrow reason. If a man would always be in a condition to think straight and to overcome a difficult or complicated situation, he should exercise his will power to control his feelings when something happens that tends to arouse his anger. An angry person cannot, as a rule, exercise leadership, unless he is dealing with people who fear his anger. Even so, permanent leadership cannot as a rule be maintained through an attitude that causes others to be afraid.

Fear.—Fear thoughts sap the strength of the will. The pessimist, the man who is constantly doubting himself, who hesitates because the possible dangers in a certain course of procedure occupy his thoughts completely, becomes the victim of a paralyzed will. The possible dangers must be looked in the face—but fearlessly. A courageous man may decide not to do a certain thing, because he sees danger that must be avoided—not because he is afraid, but because it is common sense to avoid them if they can be avoided without undue sacrifice. But he faces the odds, whatever they may be, if they must be overcome to succeed. Unlike the man whose heart is full of fear, the man of courage sees the possibility of success. His mind is full of success thoughts, not of thoughts of failure; he sees advantages in their true proportions and does not magnify disadvantages.

The salesman who has fits of blues, periods of mental depression, is giving way to fear thoughts that will surely undermine his will and may eventually unfit him for succeeding at anything. Many persons' lives are made wretched because they are constantly fearing that some calamity may happen. They fear that the house will burn; that the fruit will be destroyed by frost, and when the trees are loaded with fruit they fear it will be ruined by insects; they fear the dry weather will ruin the crops and when the rain comes they fear it will be too wet. Not only are such people unhappy themselves, they also take the joy out of life for their families and associates.

———

HABIT

6. Influence of Habit.—Habits are formed by repetition. A thing becomes easier the oftener it is done, until it is second nature and is performed without the slightest conscious effort. People walk, talk, and work, with no effort of will. Habit makes one go through certain emotions automatically; habit enables a person to take shorthand notes with great speed. A change takes place in the nerve cells each time we think. Just as a stream cuts and files its way down through the rocks, just so does a habit tend to make a path in the plastic brain; and the longer the habit is continued, the deeper becomes the path.

When a habit is formed, to do the thing is easier than to omit doing it; otherwise practice would not make perfect. Habit very early becomes a part of man's life. All through life it guides him; in fact, it may be truthfully said that man is a bundle of habits. Carlyle has truly said: "Habit is the deepest law of human nature. It is our supreme strength, if also, in certain circumstances, our miserablest weakness."

Oliver Wendell Holmes used to say: "Habit is a labor-saving invention that enables a man to get along with less fuel." Habit is one of the greatest blessings a man can have, for it enables him to perform a great deal of his daily labors without conscious attention, leaving his mind free for the things that demand voluntary attention. The best thing about habit is that a man may cultivate good habits, such as the study habit, the happiness habit, the habit of thoroughness, etc., until these things become part of his character; then to be studious, energetic, happy, thorough, etc., is easier than to be indolent, pessimistic, or lax, and one's work is done with a speed and results that astonish other men. More fortunate still, when the life is well filled with useful habits and the energies are turned into good channels there is little room for evil habits and less temptation to acquire them. The adage about mischief and crime being only misdirected energy has much sound sense in it.

7. Importance of Useful Mental Habits.—Correct physical habits, such as correct carriage, correct speech, and good manners are acquired in early youth. Mental habits are formed ordinarily in the period between twenty and thirty. If the physical habits are right, all the energy can be directed toward the right mental habits. A very important point in education is that our mental habits should lead to greater effectiveness with less effort.

One of the first habits to fix is that of self-development. If the memory is to be improved, a consistent plan must be followed every day of the week. The will power must be exercised to carry out this determination to make the effort. If a person's mind is unimaginative and barren, this defect can be overcome by a consistent course of reading and lectures.

If a person's observing powers are poor, he must conscientiously keep his eyes open. He must plan definitely to make a series of some sort of observations each day. So long as a good habit of observation is started, the kind of observation is at first immaterial. The person should become interested in some phase of science, business, or philosophy. The more he observes, the more facts he acquires, and the larger the volume of facts, the greater will become the observing powers.

The mind is capable of far greater exertion than most people imagine. Besides sleep, it needs only occasional change to overcome weariness. Everybody means to do certain things later on when he has more time; but he keeps putting them off indefinitely. He forgets that the mind must be exercised regularly all along. If this rule is not heeded, mental stagnation eventually supervenes. If people would only begin at once upon the great things they are reserving for the future, what wonders they could accomplish through the law of habit!

When he understands the power of habit for evil or good, a man should uproot his evil habits and cultivate good ones instead. This assertion is not mere preaching; it is sound business advice. No man can obtain what he is entitled to get out of business life when he is hampered with evil habits that dissipate his attention and his energies. While the man who has allowed a faulty habit to cut its channel deep in his mind may know of its existence, that knowledge is not enough. He must shake off the habit by the same means that he acquired it; that is, by properly directed repetition of the better thing that is to replace the injurious habit. The man who has spent an idle youth can, by constant work, develop the habit of industry. The ill-tempered man can develop a better temper by constant repetition of forced good humor, which finally will become a habit. The man who has allowed vulgar habits of address to become fixed upon him can, by constant repetition, bring himself up to a good standard. Constant repetition makes the change. Habit works just as strongly for the individual as against him. Patience is required in uprooting and forming habits. Six months, a year, or several years should not be grudged in the overcoming of a faulty habit and the acquisition of a good one.

In so far as men are all bundles of habits, they should aim at those that will make them most efficient. Just as people become experts in certain lines of science or business by the separate and successive hours of correct work, so they become failures by the separate and successive hours of wrong habits. No act is, strictly speaking, entirely wiped out; so every act, whether good or bad, large or small, has a part in character formation. Consequently each day men are shaping their destinies according to the kind of habits they form. The indifferent man is helping to make a habit of unfinished endeavor. The worst effect of allowing an opportunity to escape is that a bad habit is started. The next opportunity will be more likely to go by unheeded. Each day diminishes a man's possibilities, and each day lessens his chance to make a different brain path. The nervous system becomes more fixed as he grows older and he cannot make a new nervous system. He cannot live his life over again.

The best effect of starting a good new habit and keeping up continued effort is that the very faculty of effort itself will accomplish other things not at first considered. An unobserving mind can become a mind full, imaginative, and resourceful. A hesitating will may become strong and determined. A person not blessed with good manners may become truly courteous. Just as surely as day follows night, the mind will expand and develop if exercised regularly and systematically, and when the crucial test comes as to the ability to undertake the great things in life, good mental habits will have fixed a man's life upon a rock that will withstand a figurative deluge.

8. Maxims of Habit.—A few general rules are to be observed that will help in forming a new habit. When trying to acquire the habit of concentrated attention to some problem at hand, all distractions that will divert the mind must be eliminated and a condition assumed that will favor concentration. This rule will apply to every new and desired habit. The student should go where no one will talk to him or interfere with his determination. He should first relax mentally and then buckle down to his problem.

The mind must not be allowed to wander for one moment. Any outside thought that may come up, such as the picnic tomorrow or the play tonight, must be banished at once. No matter if the student must make dozens of attempts to return to the subject his mind is struggling with, he must persevere. No exception must occur until the new habit is fixed. The same course must be followed when trying to develop good common sense or self-control. The student must force his attention back to his aim until he falls easily into the habit of common sense and self-control. If he is deficient in reasoning, he must go over each step of his problem repeatedly.

He will not jump at conclusions if he has gained the necessary mental poise.

To start on a new habit is not always easy, but the one inevitable rule is to start at once. Advantage should be taken of the first chance to form a new habit. The way to correct lack of concentration is to keep the wits from wool-gathering. The student may begin at once, by concentrating on this textbook. The way to form a habit of accuracy is to be accurate now. The way to develop a purpose is to acquire some purpose right now.

9. Franklin's Method of Habit Formation. — Benjamin Franklin, inventor, statesman, writer, publisher and economist, relates in his autobiography that early in his life he decided to make a definite venture at arriving at moral perfection. He made a list of thirteen virtues, allotting a page to each. Under each virtue he wrote a precept that gave it fuller meaning. Then he practiced each one for a certain length of time. He ruled the pages into spaces and checked off each day some particular fault that he had not overcome to his satisfaction. He says that he carried out this personal examination for years. In order to do the work thoroughly he decided to attempt each virtue in the order of its importance—one at a time. He began with temperance, which included the moderating of every pleasure or inclination to develop undesirable habits, because temperance "tends to procure that coolness and clearness of head that is so necessary where constant vigilance is to be kept up and guard maintained against the unremitting attraction of ancient habits and the force of perpetual temptations."

The other virtues practiced in succession by Franklin were silence, order, resolution, frugality, industry, sincerity, justice, moderation, cleanliness, tranquility, chastity, humility. . For the precept *order* he followed a little scheme of employing his time each day. From five to seven each morning he spent in bodily personal attention, saying a short prayer, thinking over the day's business and resolutions, studying, and breakfasting. From eight till twelve he worked at his trade. From twelve to one he read or overlooked his accounts and dined. From two to five he worked at his trade. The rest of the evening until ten he spent in music, or diversion of some sort. This time was used also to put things in their places, and the last thing before retiring was the examination of the day. At the age of seventy-nine, he ascribed his health to temperance; the acquisition of his fortune to industry and frugality; the confidence of his country to sincerity and justice.

MEMORY

IMPORTANCE OF A GOOD MEMORY

10. The value to a salesman of a good memory is so obvious that it would be superfluous to present an extended argument in favor of memory training. It is sufficient to note that the salesman who remembers his customers' names and faces, the facts about the goods, or service, he is selling, the circumstances of previous interviews or sales, the rules of the house he represents, the principles and methods of correct salesmanship, as well as many other things that pertain directly, or indirectly, to his work, has a great advantage over the salesman who is notorious for having a poor memory.

Any person of average intelligence can have a good memory. But most persons' memories are not efficient. Everybody remembers certain things easily, but finds it hard to recall others. The things we remember easily are those in which we are most interested and those which have, for some reason, made deep impressions upon our minds.

Fortunately, the person who has a poor memory is not without hope of improving his ability to recall past thoughts and events; and it is the purpose here to outline briefly how a person can strengthen his memory.

FUNDAMENTAL PRINCIPLES

CONTROL OF THE SENSES

11. There are certain fundamental principles that underlie the operation and the action of the memory which must be considered in memory improvement. There are two distinct processes in remembering. First, there must be an impression made upon the mind. Then, one must have the ability to recall the impression at will. These two things must always take place in memory, and the problem of memory training is to know how to accomplish these two things.

We have five contacts with the outside world. These we call the five senses—sight, hearing, taste, smell, and touch. The nerves through which we receive impressions go to certain brain centers, and there record the various impressions they receive. Then we have memory of these things according to the avenue through which we received the impression, the memory of how an object looked, tasted, smelled, sounded, or felt.

We have control over these senses to a very marked degree, though it is a fact that the great majority of people have not cultivated that control as they might. One illustration of how one may develop and control the senses is noted in the case of the blind; it is often remarked that the fingers become eyes for the person who does not see; that is, the memory of sense impressions is highly developed. The same is true of the deaf person who has to depend upon the eyes so largely. Many impressions which the person with good hearing gets through the ears, the deaf must get through the eyes.

Every person who has a good memory uses three principles, even though he may be entirely unaware of their existence. These principles are (1) attention, (2) repetition, and (3) association.

ATTENTION

12. Importance of Strict Attention.—It is necessary that we concentrate and focus the mind upon the things we wish to remember. The mind might be likened to the sensitized photographic plate upon which impressions are made. As a good or poor light causes clear or obscure impressions to be made upon the photographic plate, so too the impressions made upon the mind are clear or indistinct, according as one is attentive or inattentive in his observations.

In emphasizing the importance of attention in remember‧ ing names, an expert in memory training related a case of an elderly man, a blacksmith, who came to him and asked if there were any simple rules that he might follow that would help him in remembering the names of the people he met. The expert said: "I told him that it should be possible for him to remember other names if he could remember his own name, his children's names, his neighbors' names, etc. He said that he had a good memory for faces, and was noted for his ability to remember the password and the ritual of his lodge. Then I said, 'All right, that is as much as we need to know; why is it that you remember these things and cannot remember some others?' Finally, I made it clear to him that the chief reason for his failure was the lack of attention, and all that he had to do in remembering names was to apply the same principle that he applied in the lodge. When the password was given to him his whole attention was directed upon that. He heard that word whispered in his ear, and nothing else. He was all attention; he knew that it would not do for him to forget this word. So, all unconscious of the fact that he was employing a great principle, he banished all other thoughts for the time and planted this one word in his mind; consequently it was a very easy matter for him to recall it at any time; then he repeated it, over and over again, each time deepening the impression upon his mind until he could not have forgotten it if he wished.

"But how about the name of the salesman he met the next morning? The man introduced himself as Mr. King. The

name was spoken much more clearly than had been the password the night before, but our friend did not pay attention;
he extended his hand and said, 'Glad to meet you; this is a
fine day, isn't it?' The fact is, he never allowed the name
to make the slightest impression upon his mind; it was never
in his mind at all. He did not repeat it, because he was more
interested in the goods he was being shown. He had in mind
price and quality rather than the salesman's name. These
things he remembered because he was interested in them, and
being interested he unconsciously concentrated his mind upon
them. If people who have poor memories will analyze their
weakness they will find that much of their trouble results
from inattention."

13. Learn to See Things Vividly.—In developing attention one should make it a point to see things clearly. The
average American is a poor observer. We go too fast to
see things distinctly; we merely get vague impressions. The
result is that we remember only a small number of the things
we see and hear. But when anything seizes our attention we
remember it. For example, if, as we are walking along the
street, there is an automobile accident, we observe it closely;
we pay attention to it; we see the cars and note many details
about them. In other words, through attention we impress
the situation on our minds so deeply that the picture is easily
and fully remembered.

It is well to note in this connection that sight is the sense
that makes the deepest impression upon the brain. Consequently we remember the things we see more readily than
things heard, smelled, tasted, or felt. The nerves connecting
the eye and the brain are much larger than the nerves connecting the brain with the other sense organs.

14. Visual Impressions the Most Accurate.—Not only
are the impressions made through the eye the strongest, but
they are also the most accurate. Therefore, the salesman
should "keep his eyes open" in reality if he wishes to improve
his memory. Some people get more benefit from travel than

others simply because they observe more closely. Their brains receive clearer impressions owing to close attention; therefore, they remember more readily and more accurately than others the scenes and events of a journey.

15. Pay Attention to Detail.—In training the memory visually, attention should be given to detail. Some automobile drivers are able to recall practically every turn in the road, tell of every interesting sight along the way, etc., because they see things in detail. An old hunter was able to glance at a flock of wild geese or ducks flying past, and turn his head away, and then count the flock simply from the picture he held in his mind's eye. He saw not only the flock, but he saw the individual birds in the flock; in other words, he saw in detail.

A salesman meeting many people should be able to remember them readily. People like to be remembered. They are pleased when one calls them by name. It is a great advantage to the salesman to be able to recognize each customer and address him by his name, but he must see the individual in detail in order to do this. Some conductors on railway trains do not use passenger checks to tab their passengers; they simply pay attention to each individual passenger, and then put him off at the proper station.

Regardless of the channel through which the impression comes to the brain, the same principle of attention should be applied as with the things we see. A person should pay attention to the things he hears, if he wishes to recall them. If he does not pay attention to the name of the person to whom he is introduced, he cannot remember it. When he hears something he wishes to remember, he should paint a mental picture of it—see it in his mind. When a speaker describes a thing or place that the listener wishes to remember, he must pay close attention to it and impress the picture upon his mind; that is, the picture that he forms through the speaker's description.

We remember unusual things because we pay attention to them. It is an uncommon thing to meet a man on the street dressed in white in the winter time. The great majority of the people we see at that time of year are dressed in dark clothes; so we would unconsciously pay attention to the individual dressed in white or any unusual color. Since we automatically pay attention to unusual things, we can often remember ordinary things or events by noting closely some characteristic or circumstance about them which is in itself out of the ordinary. We meet a person of usual height, weight, appearance, dress, etc.; but he may have a wart on his face, may wear a red tie, may have very blue eyes, or in some small detail stand out in our mind as different from other people. Only close observation will enable us, however, to pick out such details as aids to the memory.

<hr>

16. Repetition Fixes the Impression.—The second principle of memory is repetition. Things repeatedly seen, heard, spoken, felt, or tasted are more easily remembered than things that have stimulated a sense organ only once. Repetition deepens the impression made upon the brain. The impression becomes more deeply fixed, as a nail struck several times becomes more deeply imbedded in the wood than it would be if it were struck only once.

A person never forgets his own name, the name of the town in which he lives, the name of his close friend or, in fact, of any other things with which he is thoroughly familiar, because by repetition they have become deeply imbedded in his mind.

If it is desired to remember a name, the following will be found helpful: First concentrate on it—pay close attention to it; then repeat it in your mind, repeat it aloud so that you may hear it through your own voice and so that your lips and throat muscles may get the "feel" of it. Then it will often be found helpful to spell it. If it is an unusual name, ask how it is spelled. Hearing a person speak his own name makes an impression on your mind; hearing some one else repeat it deepens the impression; then if you speak the name yourself, you make the impression deeper still. The impression will also be stronger if you write the name.

17. Recalling Happenings of the Day.—In developing memory, and mental strength in general, it will be found helpful occasionally to stop and recall voluntarily things in their logical order. Some of the people of ancient times practiced a system of mind training that was very effective, but it fell into disuse largely because of printing and modern conveniences, which relieved the mind of much of its burden.

It was a form of repetition. The child was taught to recite the whole day's work. Every little detail of the day was brought out, then the events of the past week and month and year were recalled; and in this way the ancient history was carried in the minds of the people. Some of our great men practiced this same system; Thurlow Weed practiced it for 40 years, and became noted for his wonderful memory. He was so accurate in every detail that no one would question his statements, even in regard to intricate business matters; and he said that it all developed from his custom of going over the day's work in the evening. Beginning with his breakfast, he mentally recited every step during the day, thinking of the letters received at the office, their contents, what was said in answer, the people who called at his office, their errands, and all the happenings of the day. Soon he was able to skip over the minor points and center his mind on the chief element of each transaction without burdening himself with the minor points.

In practicing this system of recalling things a person should begin with himself. It is a good idea to throw everything off the mind just before retiring at night by sitting down, relaxing, and then calling in review before the mind's eye everything that has happened during the day. This may be done as follows: Begin with the first thought that entered the mind in the morning. Think what you did first after you awoke. What did you do before breakfast? What did you have for breakfast? What was the first item in the morning paper to catch your eye? What did you do immediately after breakfast? Whom did you see on your way to your place of business? Did you talk to any one? If so, what was the subject of conversation? What was the first thing you did upon entering your office? When did you go to lunch? Did you have company?

Continue the review throughout the day, right up to the last moment. You will doubtless be surprised if you have never done this to find how readily you recall very minor happenings after you have practiced this kind of concentration a little while.

On this point a store manager who conducted a training class for his salesman, said: "I have followed the practice in training retail salesmen of asking a clerk all about a certain customer he had waited on sometime during the day, and getting him to tell me as much as possible about the customer, and any noticeable characteristics he possessed; about the transaction—the goods he bought, the quality, amount, price, and the whole setting of the sale. The salesman would carefully note the customer he was waiting on just because he knew that I might ask him something about it later, and consequently he showed a surprising improvement in his work."

ASSOCIATION

18. The "Hitching Post" of Memory.—When a certain thing comes to the mind the tendency is to think of something connected with it. The first word of a line of poetry suggests the next. The words of a song suggest the music; the music suggests the words. This association of ideas is the third principle of memory training. For illustration, and for emphasis, association is sometimes spoken of as the "hitching-post" of memory, because through association we tie things together. The operation of this principle is noticeable in the working of the memory of the elderly person. Go to the old grandmother, 85 years of age, and ask her when a certain event with which she is supposed to be familiar happened. It may have been a half century or more ago; but the chances are she will have "hitching-posts" along the way to which she has tied things that enable her to recall the event accurately. She will likely start by saying, "Well, now let me see. John was born on a certain date, or that was just before the year of the big flood," etc.

We associate things in three ways; namely, (*a*) by likeness, (*b*) by contrast, (*c*) by concurrence.

19. Likeness.—We associate readily things that are alike or have a common characteristic; as, rich man—Rockefeller; wise man—Solomon. We remember a stranger because he resembles, in some way, a friend or an acquaintance; he has the same complexion, build or mannerisms. His name may be associated with some peculiarity of the man himself. A very tall man by the name of Gear could be remembered by thinking of him as high Gear. A man of dark complexion by the name of Brown could be associated with his dark skin. A person by the name of Carroll could be put down as a possible singer (of carols) and remembered in that way. One by the name of Stanley could be thought of as one who is a great traveler, and by association with the name of the explorer, Stanley. It is not enough for us to know that this is true, but we must train the mind to grasp and apply these things of its own accord. This comes by practice. We should look for similarities between the new thing and something already familiar, as an aid in recalling people and objects, places, and dates.

20. Contrast.—We associate things by contrast; as, hot-cold, rich-poor. We think of the short man in contrast with the tall, the fat with the lean, the old with the young, the mechanic with the business man. We see an automobile pass our door and think of its being like our own, but of a different color. We must learn to apply these contrasts—make them work for our own mind, have them at command.

21. Concurrence.—The third attribute of association is concurrence. On thinking of rough rider, the mind immediately flashes to Roosevelt; the thought of San Juan Hill brings up rough rider, and then president; on thinking of White House, a whole train of thoughts are awakened. Columbus brings to mind America. The United States flag displayed from the top of a building makes one think of Washington, of the Fourth of July, of the minute men, of the British soldiers, perhaps of Mount Vernon and the Potomac River, and so on; Wellington and Napoleon recall Waterloo, by the concurrence. The same process can be applied to our own surroundings and to our business. Our minds should be able to flash before us the thoughts of a certain customer, in relation to his business or a particular event. These should lead to a special suit of clothes or farm implement or barrel of sugar that he bought. A man's name should recall other things and give a clew to the whole situation in dealing with him again.

_____

ACCURACY OF MEMORY

22. Many persons say that they have a good memory, but it is slow and they always must have time to think in order to be absolutely sure of a thing. But such a memory is of comparatively little practical value to one engaged in business where the principles of leadership must be applied, as in selling.

The salesman's memory should always be both quick and accurate; and the person who finds that his memory is inclined to be slow and inaccurate will find that he can overcome the weakness, at least to a very great extent, by exercising care, that is, close attention, in his thinking. An inaccurate memory is usually the result of carelessness or indifference upon the part of the individual in securing mental impressions. When you meet a person who says, "I think thus and so, but now I really am not sure about it," you are usually correct in suspecting that such a person is not careful in his thinking. Such persons may be able to get things straight in their minds after thinking a while, but they always lack vim and snap. In short, they lack the kind of impressiveness that a clear, quick, accurate memory gives. Thinking of a big black dog makes a deeper impression upon the mind than merely thinking of a dog, and the memory is more accurate in recalling the object.

Many salesmen make the mistake of speaking of their goods as "things" or "stuff." Every piece of merchandise, every article handled by the salesman, has a name and the salesman strengthens himself, and deepens the impression made upon the mind of the customer, when he uses exact terms in presenting his proposition. The law of memory operates in the case of the customer just as it does with the salesman; and the salesman should always endeavor to make an impression upon the mind of the customer that will be both favorable and lasting.

POINTS TO OBSERVE IN MEMORY TRAINING

23. The following points should be kept in mind in connection with memory training:

1. A person should store his mind with the greatest possible number of good and useful things. He should observe everything attentively.

2. The mind should be trained to remember, or recall, things at command with the greatest possible accuracy and rapidity, and with the least possible effort.

3. A certain amount of mechanical drill is necessary in memorizing. A lesson must be gone over repeatedly until it is recalled easily. Facts of importance that must be on the tip of the tongue must be repeated at intervals until they come almost automatically to mind when needed.

4. The less the effort required to remember, the greater will be the individual's power of leadership, as the greater will be the time that can be utilized in advance thinking.

5. The greater the accuracy and certainty of the memory the less the chance of failure—and the less chance of failure the greater the chance of success.

6. The memorizing of a certain thing is best distributed over a number of attempts on succeeding days. The drill should be extended over a long, rather than a short, period of time. In this way it will be more thoroughly retained.

7. To retain a thing for a long period, it is necessary, first, to concentrate on it thoroughly and recall it often until it is permanently fixed in the memory.

8. All possible helps should be utilized. The student may repeat his data to himself, may repeat them aloud, may discuss them with others, and may commit them to writing.

It is a wonderful thing to have a memory so well trained that one can, as it were, press the button and have this servant before him instantaneously with the object he wants. And this is possible, and practical, too, for the average person. The laws of memory are positive and not difficult to master. If a person's memory is not good he should at once begin to put into practice these simple principles which will enable him to increase his power of memory. This power is especially effective in one's work as a salesman.

ABILITY TO TALK

GOOD GENERAL KNOWLEDGE

24. The successful salesman must be able to talk well, but at the same time he should be careful not to say too much. Everything he says should be to some purpose. Mere chattering does not win orders; there should be a real message behind the talk, which must be clear cut and to the point. The man who believes in his work and primes himself with an enthusiastic knowledge of it is not likely to have serious difficulty in talking interestingly and convincingly. But he can always talk more smoothly and to the point when he has gone over the ground beforehand.

A salesman to be a good talker has need of a greater stock in trade than knowledge of his proposition. To grow up to his full measure of effectiveness and to command respect and confidence, he must keep himself well informed by the reading of a carefully selected list of good newspapers, magazines, and books. Nowadays the literature of business is growing rapidly in volume. Business topics are discussed in many magazines of general circulation, while publications especially devoted to various kinds of business are increasing in number, influence, and interest. Many books on various business subjects are published every year, and a wealth of worthwhile information is readily available to the salesman who desires to keep in touch with the latest thought in business and in his particular field of selling. Records of the Library of Congress show that up to 1900 only eleven books on Salesmanship had been published in this country, but in the next 25 years over 400 books on Salesmanship were published, and during the past few years they have been coming out at the rate of more than fifty books a year.

A salesman who is equipped with a fund of general knowledge is often able in the course of a business talk to advance some point that is new to the other. We are likely to think of the things we know as common, but when we hear a thing that we do not know, we think of the person who told us as being above the ordinary, and accordingly we find it easy to repose confidence in him. We are always attracted by the fascinating stories told by the traveler; he is able to tell us things we do not know. The salesman should remember this and, the next time he is selling something, should make it a point to tell the customer something that he does not know about it. This will give him confidence in the salesman's ability to advise him. He is a poor salesman who, selling steam shovels, does not keep informed on the biggest news of the engineering world, who will look blank when some one speaks of certain notable features of the Panama Canal or of a celebrated subway work under progress. One solicitor for an engineering magazine, before making his calls, regularly obtains from the editors of his publication information on the developments and opportunities in certain lines. As he reads a certain amount of industrial news constantly, so as to be on common ground with the technical men he meets, he is able to command their confidence. The cash-register and the adding-machine salesman must be well informed on modern business systems. The drug salesman must know the latest developments in drug markets and legislation.

CONSIDERING THE LISTENER'S VIEWPOINT

25. Interest in Person Addressed.—Naturally, the salesman's primary object is to be able to talk well on his own subject, and yet no man ever became a good talker without training himself to talk on subjects that are of interest to others and to take an interest in other men's affairs. Good conversation can never be a one-sided affair, and confidence is gained by a proper consideration of the other man taking part in the interchange of thoughts and opinions. A good salesman makes it his business to find out what his prospect is most interested in and he keeps these interests prominent in the conversation. Many of his remarks are in the form of questions—questions that do not antagonize nor show undue curiosity, but that stimulate the listener to indicate fully his needs and problems. The good salesman realizes that he cannot win the confidence of those whom he addresses unless he considers their point of view and adapts his canvass to that point of view. Many salesmen can credit a big order to their ability to discover a man's interests and to talk to him about them. The man who lacks a real interest in his customer's affairs, who pretends to be interested only in order to secure attention for himself will sooner or later reveal his insincerity. The salesman cannot achieve lasting success as long as he is selfish in his thinking and talking.

26. Ability to Listen Well.—Every salesman knows how he feels when another man rudely interrupts his conversation and shows that he gives little consideration to what others say. Let him, therefore, carefully guard against such disregard of his prospect's feelings and remember that the ability to talk well includes the quality of being a good listener.

The salesman in his enthusiam regarding the merits of his proposition should bear in mind that talking too aggressively will bore the prospect. So instead of airing his opinions with a long uninterrupted discussion of his goods, the tactful salesman says a few sentences and then gives the person addressed an opportunity to talk. This will not only be taken as a compliment by the prospect but will readily give the salesman a chance to direct his own reply properly, provided he has listened courteously and attentively. When a prospect has a good chance to express his ideas he will give some hint to the salesman as to the proper arguments to use and how to present them so that they will be in accord with the thinking habits of the prospect. If the prospect talks quickly, uses few words and shows the ability to absorb a point readily, naturally the salesman gives his canvass in concise form along the lines in which the prospect displays interest. On the other hand, it may be found that the prospect is a slow thinker and requires a detailed description of the goods. Or the salesman may be canvassing a farmer who is not familiar with the same general forms of expression as the college professor, the doctor, or the lawyer. In order to make his conversation most effective the salesman should know much about the people he meets in order to select words and expressions that appeal to them. Therefore he should encourage the prospect to take part in the conversation, and remember that a good talker is a good listener, and a good conversation is a mutual exchange of opinions, not a monologue.

THE ART OF TACTFUL PERSUASION

27. In talking business it must be borne in mind that one can rarely win another, that is, cause him to change an opinion, by direct argument with him. It is necessary to agree first with him on at least one point, and then gradually lead him to one's own way of thinking. As one sales manager expresses it, "You lock arms with your prospect instead of locking horns with him." For example, if the salesman wants a man to walk east with him, but the man wants to walk west, the salesman should not knock him down and drag him east. Instead he should lock arms with him and walk west with him a block, then turn the corner north or south, and after a while swing around the corner to the east. Before the man realizes it he is walking the salesman's way. To illustrate the operation of this principle suppose a prospect who is considering the purchase of a real-estate bond says that rentals are going down, and therefore real-estate bonds don't look like a very good investment.   Instead of directly opposing his argument, the salesman could say, "Yes, that may be true in some cases.   I know of one instance where office-building rentals have been reduced 10 per cent. but the margin of income over the amount necessary to pay interest on these bonds is so great that even if rentals are reduced, the interest is always sure to be paid promptly, and so the desirability of these bonds is not lessened."   In this way the salesman has succeeded in meeting the prospect's objection without directly opposing his point of view.

The secret of ability to win and lead others by the personal appeal, is in the ability to employ tact in approaching these feelings, prejudices, and opinions.   It is like steering a boat around a dangerous point; it is easily done when one knows just where the point is, but if the captain is not experienced he is apt to run squarely against the obstacle that is just below the surface.   So in conversation if one can draw the other out just enough to show where the shallow places and the rocks are one can easily avoid them.

GOOD ENGLISH

28.   Importance of Correct Speech.—In the section entitled *The Salesman's Language* there is a detailed discussion of common errors in speech, of the study of words, and of clearness, force, and harmony—the fundamental qualities of a good style of expression.   This section should be used constantly for reference purposes.

Nothing is so quickly noticed in the general expression of a stranger, by the cultured person, as incorrect English; so common errors in grammar should be studiously guarded against by any one who hopes to become an effective talker. If a salesman says "them things" for "those things," "hain't" for "is not," "ain't worth nothing" for "is not worth anything," some of the persons he talks to will be very unfavorably impressed.   A great deal of nonsense is talked about the needlessness of using good English. It is true that in some instances a man may make grammatical blunders without loss to himself, but it is certain that he is never helped by them and that in some lines of work errors of speech are a real hindrance. If one is not absolutely certain of the exact meaning and of the correct pronunciation of a word, it is better by far not to use it. However, every salesman should make a constant effort to improve his vocabulary. A little review will enable him to weed out the common errors and thus make him more at ease when talking to educated people. Good reading does much toward improving one's store of language and teaching the correct use of words. Association with good talkers also helps. The dictionary should be freely used in looking up the meaning and pronunciation of words. Every word added to the vocabulary serves either to increase one's range of thought, or to improve one's power of expression.

It is well for a person to question himself on this point and learn just how broad and flexible a vocabulary he has. If he were describing a piece of goods of any kind, is he sure that he could use the proper words in every case? If he were describing a building, could he use the correct architectural terms? Could he distinguish between a tower and a minaret and a turret? If he were talking about a ship could he express his thoughts intelligently? Or if he were conversing on any one of a hundred subjects that he might mention, could he use just the right words in expressing the thoughts he might wish to convey?

29. Cautions as to the Use of Words.—In regard to the use of words, it is well to offer a few cautions:

1. Avoid unfamiliar words. Always try to express your thoughts in the everyday vocabulary of the average man. This to a great extent is the secret of the success of eminent lecturers and orators, popular short-story writers and successful politicians. A careful study of great speeches, like Lincoln's Gettysburg address, shows that their strength lies largely in the use of plain unpretentious words, easily understood by any one with an ordinary education.

2. Avoid the use of localisms. Localisms are words used in certain localities only, and therefore not understood, or differently understood, in other localities. Under this head are included words like these: Tote (carry), reckon (think), tuckered (tired), near (in the sense of stingy).

3. Use the utmost discretion in the use of slang. Some people believe that slang ought to be avoided altogether, but that is a foolish idea, because some slang terms are so expressive that nothing else can take their place. For example, such expressions as "make good," "get busy," etc., which may be considered slang would probably be more effective in a selling talk than any substitutes that could be found for them. The proper principle to follow in the use of slang is to avoid, always, slang expressions that are vulgar and likely to make an unfavorable impression upon the listener.

4. Avoid phrases that have been used so much that they lack effectiveness. Some persons who religiously avoid slang expressions, freely use hackneyed phrases, not realizing that by so doing they are not only showing mental laziness by using the ideas of others, but are also making their talk unemphatic by their lack of individuality. Some examples of stereotyped phrases that are commonly heard are: "As far as that is concerned," "You know," "In the last analysis," "Of course," etc.

5. Avoid technical terms. Technical words are such as are clearly understood only by persons of a single class or profession. Such words should be used only when it is certain that they will be understood by the listener. Examples of technical words are dielectric, anode, ampere, volt, and ohm (electrical terms), tort, escheat, duress, venue, and replevin (legal terms), quoin, pica, em, and matrix (printing terms).

USING THE VOICE EFFECTIVELY

30. Value of a Pleasing Voice.—It is obvious that one who is to do his work, to some extent at least, by the use of his voice has a distinct advantage if he has a pleasant, clear voice. It is not necessary to attend a school of elocution, but every salesman should give attention to cultivating a pleasant voice. Men differ greatly in their voices. One man will be so loud or raspy in his conversation that he will be irritating to many with whom he comes in contact. The boisterous, rough talker is a very common type. At the other extreme is a man who talks so low or who mumbles so that it is difficult to understand him. Then there are those who talk too rapidly or too slowly for the best effect.

Some are naturally gifted with voices of unusual clearness and melody. The pleasing tone of the voices of many actors, actresses, and public speakers is a subject of common comment, and is no small factor of their popularity.

One of the greatest voice trainers of America said: "The ambition to have a voice that one can throw to the farthest corner of the greatest hall is no mean one. Truth has wings when a finely vibrating voice, warmed by a healthy blood flow, paints it with all the glorious colors of burning passion. To hear the fine swells of some great actor's voice, as it grows with his theme is impressive, electrifying; to be that orator is magnificent."

It is well for the salesman's success to possess in some degree these qualities. He can have them if he will work for them, and it is very essential that the salesman have a good voice, a voice that he can control and into which he can throw considerable feeling if need be.

There are not a few instances on record showing that sometimes one may possess a powerful personality when the voice is the only redeeming feature. One of the most notable of these is that of the deposed Sultan of Turkey, Abdul-Hamid, who was noted as one of the most heartless and unscrupulous rulers that ever sat upon a throne; he apparently had no conscience and did not stop at anything to accomplish his desires. He was hated and feared by all who had occasion to know his power. But in spite of all his weaknesses and repulsive nature he possessed a remarkable voice and those who were close to him in his days of power say that it was his voice that made it possible for him to hold his throne as long as he did. Wicked and heartless as was this man it is said that his voice possessed a pathetic quality that would soften the most heartless. Many an enemy has met Abdul-Hamid with the firm resolve to take him prisoner, but has been dissuaded by this wonderful quality of voice; and statesmen who disagreed with him on policies of state invariably came from his presence won over to his views, though they knew deep down in their hearts that he was insincere in what he said. It was the pathos, music, rhythm, and clearness of his voice that so completely won and captivated his enemies and charmed his friends. It is said that toward the close of his career upon the throne, diplomatists from other nations refused to meet Abdul-Hamid face to face, but when it was necessary for them to transact business with him they did it through subordinates simply to avoid the charm of his voice.

31. How to Develop the Voice.—While it may not be possible for every person to develop a voice of unusual attractiveness, any one, with care, can overcome decided faults. For example, if a man, on asking friends, finds that his fault is loud or harsh talking, he can take care to subdue his voice. At home, where there is more freedom in criticizing such faults, is a good place to be reminded of what needs correcting, and to practice better tones. The object should be to cultivate a clear, mellow tone.

The first secret of a good voice is proper breathing. This means that the breath must not only be deep and full, but it must be properly controlled. The principal voice muscles in breathing are those of the abdomen; the breath should be forced through the oral cavity by these muscles, which force the diaphragm upwards. A splendid exercise to accomplish this consists in blowing through a quill. The power to control the breath is one of the principal factors in proper breathing, and it will be noticed that, in blowing the breath through a quill or a pipe stem, the muscles of the abdomen become hard and rigid. Another very good exercise for strengthening these muscles lies in pronouncing the words, *Who-Hup-Hah*, making them short and in quick succession.

To open the throat, use the following exercise: Prolong the sounds *E-A-O-Ah*. Start on the *"E"* sound, open the mouth a little wider and continue the *"A,"* then make the mouth perfectly round and sound the *"O,"* and finally change to the *"Ah."* Do not be afraid to practice these simple little exercises with earnestness. If you were to take a two years' course in voice training you would be compelled to practice these same simple exercises every day. But as you practice them remember that you are doing it for a purpose. That purpose is to develop the organs of speech and the muscles that control them so that it becomes natural for them to act properly.

32. Practice Speaking Distinctly.—It is not only a great injustice to oneself, but it is too much to ask of a customer to compel him continually to ask the salesman to repeat himself. The salesman's voice should be under such perfect control that others hear clearly every word he says. If he speaks too fast or mumbles, he must train himself to pronounce his words more deliberately. Reading aloud is good practice for developing distinct pronunciation. To learn to speak distinctly one should practice over and over words and expressions that have a tendency to keep the throat open, and words that express various sentiments that one has to deal with in influencing people. The following exercises are helpful: Practice saying the word *warm* over and over many times —make it warm, make others feel the warmth of it; keep the throat open and make the word just as big and round as possible. Look into a mirror and go through the motions of making the word without sound. The idea is to develop the muscles of the throat and face until it becomes natural for them to form such words.

Practice the word *one*. Repeat it. Give different meanings to it. Make it full and round as in the simple statement *"One"*; then make it again as a command quick and sharp.

One of the greatest faults in the voice is the dropping of the palate; it is often inclined to hang too low and thus obstruct the air passage. This of course has a tendency to make the voice indistinct. To overcome this, open the mouth wide and prolong the sound *"Ah."* Don't be afraid to make it big and full and free. You can practice this exercise until the throat becomes open and remains so; and it should be borne in mind that the voice cannot be clear, ringing, and magnetic unless this passage is open and well-formed.

To make yourself easily understood practice such words as the following. Make every sound perfectly distinct; do not slight any part of the word. It is the ability to pronounce distinctly every syllable of the word that makes one easily understood. Do not slight your words, especially by dropping the last syllable or the last letter. Many people are inclined to blur their words by running letters and syllables together. But careful practice of the following words will remedy this defect. There are, of course, a great many words that might be added to this list. You can add words as they occur to you. Practice this list until you have thoroughly mastered every combination:

Cribb'd, Bobb'd, Cribb'dst, Troubles, Bubbles, Ambl'd, Rumbl'd, Bright, Brow, Bridge, Nibs, Ribs.

Kindl'd, Fiddl'd, Handl'dst, Widths, Breadths, Seas'n'd, Reas'n'd, Emblaz'n'st.

Stifl'd, Muffl'd, Tough'n, Rough'n, Freak, Frank, Frisk, Fifths, Twelfths, Lift'st.

Sparkl'd, Circl'd, Shackl'd'st, Weak'n'd, Wields, Shields, Shelf's, Gulf's, Elm, Whelm, Realms, Films, Shalt, Quilt, Resolv'st, Solv'st.

Nymphs, Trumps, Prompt'st, Long, Lingering, Lengths, Reveng'd, Plung'd, Rant, Mint, Dimpl'd, Sharp'n'd.

Barb, Suburb, Curb, Girds, Herds, Serge, Verge, Gorge, Nerves, Serves, Asks, Masques, Frisks, Shrill, Shrive, Shrunk.

Splendor, Spleen, Grasps, Lisps, Hast, Cast, Thrill, Thrice, Throb, Trowel, Tremble, Received, Rav'd, Shovel'd, Driv'ls, Bev'ls, Ev'ls.

MEMORY HELPS

He who can answer the following questions from memory has a good under-standing of the text in the preceding pages.

(1)   What rules should be observed in forming a new habit?

(2)   How can detrimental habits be uprooted?

(3)   How does habit help one?

(4)   Define *will*.

(5)   What is the value of a well-trained will?

(6)   What is the difference between will power and stubbornness?

(7)   How can desire be crystallized into will?

(8)   Why is decision an important quality for a salesman to develop?

(9)   In developing decision what caution should be kept in mind?

(10)   What is the relation of confidence to will power?

(11)   What things should be avoided in developing will power?

(12)   In what ways is a good memory helpful to a salesman?

(13)   Why is it easier to remember things seen than things heard?

(14)   In what three ways do we associate things?

(15)   How can a salesman improve his vocabulary?

(16)   What principle should be observed in using slang?

(17)   (*a*) What are some common faults in regard to the use of the voice?
(*b*) Explain how these faults can be corrected.

(18)   How can the salesman overcome the habit of speaking indistinctly?

PHYSICAL EFFICIENCY

HEALTH

INTRODUCTION

1. When the human body acts in a normal manner and there is nothing present to irritate or destroy it in any way, each organ functioning properly, there exists a bodily condition known as health. In other words, health is the result when the body works under favorable and natural conditions.

Bodily health is the logical starting point of self-development. So necessary is it that no man in his senses will long disregard it, more especially a salesman. In order to do his most effective work, the salesman needs good health—a vigorous, cheerful vitality. The man of unusually strong character may have a will powerful enough to spur him on to great efforts, despite the fact that he is physically weak, but good physique is a most valuable asset in selling work and one to be guarded with great care. Those who enjoy good health do not always appreciate that health is wealth, and act as if the body may be abused with impunity. While many people give themselves needless concern about their health and become eccentric or morbid on the subject, a larger number think little about the care of their bodies. Because they can do certain things without apparent injury, they take liberties with physical laws and sometimes boast of the excesses they can endure. It is an excellent thing to have a constitution that is proof against many of the ills of mankind; but caution must be exercised lest the limit of endurance be reached without warning.

The traveling salesman, subjected to alternate periods of labor and leisure, obliged to travel constantly, and being very irregular in regard to sleeping and eating, is likely to have his efficiency lowered by the irregularities of his work. He should, therefore, know how to keep in good physical condition. A large number of sales will hinge on his appearance, and appearance is largely dependent on health. Further, his work is a constant matching of wits with the buyer, and whatever his feelings, he must always be aggressive; therefore, he must be in perfect physical condition, if he hopes to get the best of the encounter.

FACTORS OF GOOD HEALTH

PROPER BREATHING

2. Importance of Proper Breathing.—Breathing is the most important function of the body. Man may live for days without food, drink, or sleep; but he can live only a few minutes without air. While the fact that a person must breathe to live is well known, few stop to learn what important functions go on during the breathing process. Oxygen is taken into the body more readily through breathing than through food, and a great deal of waste is thrown off when the breath is expelled. Through the respiratory tract the air reaches the lungs, where oxygen is absorbed into the system to enrich the blood and to aid in renewing the worn-out tissue of the body, and in exchange carbonic acid and other waste matter are thrown off with the expired air. This interchange occurs in the minute air cells, of which the lungs are composed. The surface represented by these little cells is so great that if spread out it would cover a space of 500 or 600 square feet. The air cells also play a very important part in some diseases; for instance, in pneumonia they become filled with the product of inflammation and air cannot enter the portion of the lung involved, and if this condition is sufficiently extensive death results. In tuberculosis, or consumption, the cells are not only rendered useless, but ultimately are destroyed, forming cavities in the lungs.

These facts teach the exceedingly important lesson that the lungs should be kept filled with fresh air, in order that all parts of these organs may be kept in a healthy and active state. In this way, the air not only reaches the cells but it also allows free exit of poisonous waste products from the tissues, and renders the lungs far more able to resist disease.

Observation has disclosed the fact that practically all despondent, downcast, and discouraged people are shallow breathers. The reason for this is that shallow breathing favors the accumulation of poisonous gases in the blood and the stagnation of blood in the internal organs. The accumulation of these poisonous gases in the blood stream becloud the mind, producing a mental and physical state that makes it much harder for one to live a happy, tranquil, and tempered life.

Deep breathing greatly heightens the brain action. Thus, deep breathers are more likely to be deep thinkers, while shallow breathers are guilty of shallow thinking. The action of the lungs affects the circulation of the blood, especially in the head and abdomen. To convince yourself that this is a fact, some time when you are all tired out, dull, and sleepy, and unable to read, put down your book for a moment, stand before an open window and slowly fill the lungs to the fullest capacity twenty-five times. On resuming your reading, you will discover a new lease of mental energy—the powers of attention have been awakened.

Deep breathing also facilitates the purification of the blood as it circulates through the lungs. It likewise quickens the circulation of the blood throughout the body. Chronic cold hands and feet are often greatly helped by systematic deep breathing.

A further benefit to be had from deep breathing is in the aid it gives to digestion. It promotes the action of the liver, and helps the stomach in emptying itself. That "heavy feeling" which is so often apparent in the stomach following meals can be relieved in 10 or 15 minutes by deep, diaphragmatic breathing in the open air. Very often headache, constipation, backache, and many other unpleasant symptoms may also be greatly helped or entirely removed by habitual, deep, diaphragmatic breathing.

3. Proper Method of Breathing.—Considering the importance of breathing and the sustenance the body derives from this act, it is surprising how few people breathe properly. Many people breathe habitually through the mouth—a bad practice. Many others take only a half breath, thus robbing the body of much of the sustenance it should have; this method is termed shallow breathing. On going into the open air, on retiring at night, on rising, and at other convenient times, every one should take a few deep breaths, so that the habit of better regular breathing will eventually be formed. The intake should always be made through the nose. One who finds it necessary to breathe through the mouth should consult a specialist at once, for obstructions in the nasal cavities, though extremely common, interfere seriously with breathing and with the health; they may, however, be removed with very little discomfort.

One of the first essentials to correct breathing is proper carriage of the body. Always stand erect and in an easy position. The old teaching was "throw the shoulders back," but this is wrong, it makes the body stiff and it cramps the lungs in the back. The proper way to control the shoulders is to think little about them *but hold the chest up*—if you will hold the chest up the shoulders will take care of themselves.

4. Breathing Exercises.—When practicing deep breathing, fresh air should be had. While standing erect the lower part of the lungs should be filled first, by making the diaphragm push out the walls of the abdomen. Then the middle portion of the lungs should be filled by distending the lower ribs and the breastbone. Finally, the upper part of the lung cavity should be inflated. The breath should then be slowly expelled. Practice inhaling in long, steady, deep breaths. While walking inhale and count five in the mind, then exhale the breath while counting five more. Count five once more before breathing again. Then begin all over and keep this up for ten minutes at a time.

A method of deep breathing followed in gymnasiums is to stand erect, with the arms hanging limp at the sides, and as the air is inhaled to raise the arms slowly until they are high above the head at the time the lungs are completely filled; then, as the arms are dropped, to expel the air quickly through the mouth.

Another exercise is to extend the arms in front of the body and, as the air is inhaled, draw the hands slowly back toward the armpits, clenching the hands as they are drawn back until the fists are tensely clenched when they reach the armpits; then, while holding the breath, slowly force the fists forwards, and draw them back with some vigor several times before vigorously expelling the air through the mouth. Persistent use of these exercises is sure to produce beneficial results.

It should be remembered that lung strength cannot be determined entirely by ability to inhale air. Often, as in the case of the public speaker, lung power is determined largely by the ability to control the breath. Practice blowing the breath through a quill, or through a small opening in your mouth, and note how tense the muscles about the abdomen become. This should be practiced over and over for the purpose of strengthening and developing these muscles.

One should always breathe pure, fresh air. Open your windows at night and let the fresh air rush in and drive out the foul air that has been in the lungs and taken up the impurities from the blood, and whenever you are out in the open, as every one should be as much as possible, make it a practice to breathe deep, full and often.

5. Ventilation.—Pure air is admittedly the greatest tonic. It is also one of the best weapons for fighting tuberculosis and other diseases. The source of many of man's ills lies in the insufficient amount of pure air that he breathes, and he cannot get too much of it. Nature designed man for more out-of-door life than a large proportion of men now enjoy. The effect of civilization is to shut people up within narrow walls for the greater part of the time and thus to deprive them of their greatest invigorator. Comparatively few schools, churches, offices, shops, stores, dwellings, or other buildings are properly ventilated.

Every working and sleeping place should have some arrangement by which foul air may gradually escape and fresh air come in, especially when a number of people occupy the room. No one should sleep in a room without opening a window enough to introduce a considerable volume of fresh air. The benefit of fresh air while sleeping is shown by the excellent effects of the open-air sleeping rooms on invalids. The number of private houses with open-air sleeping rooms is constantly increasing.

If a working place has no provision for regular ventilation, the windows should always be opened a little to provide a quantity of fresh air. Employes cannot always have proper ventilation of their working places, because its importance is not sufficiently understood by employers or those in charge of the buildings. Furthermore, many people are so much alarmed when fresh air is felt that they prefer to breathe air that is sometimes so foul as to be actually offensive to one coming in from the outside.

PROPER EATING

6. Overeating.—To the subject of dietetics has been given a great deal of consideration during late years. Sanitariums, hospitals, and laboratories have conducted elaborate and extensive experiments to determine the value of foods, and many works reporting the findings of such experiments have been published. But after all is said, the one notable and outstanding fact is that, so far as real personal efficiency is concerned, common sense on the part of the individual is of paramount consideration, and the following paragraphs dealing briefly with the subject of proper eating should enable one to grasp readily the principles involved and apply them to his individual case.

Men in all walks of life continually eat more than is good for them. Fortunately, a growing class of housekeepers believe that eating is not the greatest thing in life and so have fewer dishes, well selected and well cooked. But millions continue to load their tables, and their idea of enjoyment is that all grown persons, as well as children, should eat as much as they can contain. Tolstoi, the great Russian, said that men feed themselves as if they were stallions rather than men.

Dr. Alvah H. Doty says: "There is good reason to believe that continued overeating is indirectly responsible for a greater loss of life than that which follows the excessive use of liquor. As a rule, we eat much more than we need. This is intemperance and leads to many unpleasant conditions. We take a large amount of food that has but little nutritive value and is often very difficult to digest. This constantly overtaxes the digestive organs, sooner or later renders them unable to perform their functions properly, and may afterwards lead to organic disease. One of the unpleasant effects of liquor is the abnormal appetite that it is apt to create, which calls for an increased and unnecessary amount of food."

An overloaded stomach means an overworked stomach. This, in turn, brings on the temptation to take drinks that will whip up the digestive action and force the work. Not only is blood that is needed by the brain taken away to the stomach, but the physical functions from the digestion down are clogged or put to severe tests. Consequently, the body is regularly in the condition of an overworked engine that may break down at any time. From childhood the appetite is, in most cases, indulged unchecked, and hence overeating becomes a habit, to be overcome only by reasoning and will. Selling is brain work principally, and men of great brain efficiency are not gluttons, but moderate eaters.

Doctor Sager says: "Simplicity in habits of eating and the avoidance of all stimulating foods are, with the exception of religion, the most powerful of all aids to purity of life. Good living is a religion in itself. Many a man is trying to do by prayer what can be acquired far more easily and naturally by correct habits of living."

Many diseases may be traced directly to overloaded stomachs and to the consequent lack of digestion. Food that is so eaten that it is properly digested, is turned into a milk-like fluid that is readily assimilated by the body. Undigested food ferments and decays and has a poisonous, instead of a nourishing, effect; thus the entire plan of digestion is upset and bodily and mental discomfort follow.

7. Rational Eating.—The subject of proper food is a broad one and one that must consider the needs of the individual. Most men can correct some abuses without advice; but every one should read some good work on rational living in order to understand how the application of a few common-sense principles in regard to diet may increase efficiency. The following suggestions have been given by competent advisers as means of correcting some common abuses.

The first requirement is *thorough mastication.* Hurried eating, which is particularly an American fault, is as deplorable as overeating. It is wrong to bolt down masses of partly masticated food, after taking only 10 or 15 minutes for a process that should last several times as long. Mr. Horace Fletcher became famous by his advocacy of the thorough chewing of food, and by his own experience and that of others proved the remarkable health- and strength-giving result of thorough mastication. *Fletcherizing* means nothing more than eating only what the appetite strenuously requires and chewing that until the food becomes a paste, thoroughly insalivated. Then swallowing is not forced, but comes as an act that can hardly be resisted. The habit of proper chewing not only permits the saliva to do its intended work, but promotes the flow of gastric juice in the stomach and thus prepares the stomach for the reception of food. The best foods on which to practice proper chewing are dry bread, crackers, zwieback—a twice-baked bread—toast, or such dried fruits as prunes. Thorough mastication serves to satisfy the appetite. The man who Fletcherizes requires only one-half the usual amount of food.

Soft, mushy foods do not lend themselves well to mastication. Hard foods are not only better for the teeth, affording them proper exercise and preventing decay, but are better from the digestive point of view. Such foods as pastry are commonly taken into the stomach only partly prepared for digestion, so that work that the mouth should do is thrown on the stomach, which is usually already abused by an overload.

Food should never be washed down with large swallows of any liquid; such procedure is only encouraging insufficient chewing and insalivation. Only a small quantity of any liquid should be taken while eating. The average American will gulp down an entire cup of coffee by the time the average European has sipped a few teaspoonfuls. The liquids taken during the meal should be sipped as if tasting. No matter how busy a man may be, he cannot use time to better advantage than in proper eating, because eating bears too close a relation to his other activities for him to neglect it.

As the process of digestion is regulated largely by the mental state, as well as by the sense of taste, special effort should be made to make the meal hour the most pleasant of the day, refraining from taxing and troublesome thoughts at this time, and devoting it to the pleasure of eating, to the intelligent gratification of appetite, and to the full and free enjoyment of the food. Let the hour at the table be one of good cheer and social intercourse.

8. Organic and Inorganic Foods.—Food is classed as organic and inorganic; organic substances are divided into those which contain nitrogen and those which do not. The organic nitrogenized substances are known as *proteids,* and are by far the most important articles of food, for nitrogen is required in the formation of new and the repair of old tissue and in the proper nourishment of the body, and without it life would soon be extinct. The proteids are well known in the forms of meat, the albumen, or white, of eggs, the casein of milk, the gluten of flour, and so on, and are specially needed to supply strength and motion.

The organic non-nitrogenized substances, as the name implies, contain no nitrogen, and are recognized in the forms of fat and sugars, the latter being known as *carbohydrates;* starches are included in this class and during the process of digestion are transformed into sugar. Sugars and fats are heat producers, besides being important agents of nutrition. If they are reduced in amount below a certain point, a condition follows that renders the person more susceptible to disease. Fat is found immediately under the skin, as well as in the deeper tissues, and, being a poor conductor, aids in retaining the warmth of the body and protects it against cold. Fat is required over parts exposed to pressure and aids in maintaining the symmetry of the body.

Organic substances, in supplying the various tissues with nourishment, lose their identity and leave the body in a changed condition or as waste matter, which is eliminated largely through the intestinal tract and the kidneys.

Inorganic substances consist of water and various salts, which are necessary to maintain properly the functions of the body. They are specially needed in connection with the various secretions, such as the gastric and intestinal juices, but, unlike organic substances, they are eliminated from the body in the same form in which they enter it.

9. Food Values.—The consideration, in a general way, of the material required to nourish the body, gives a better understanding of the value of various articles of food, particularly under special conditions. For instance, an athlete, while in training, does not use fat as a diet, for it would increase his weight and would add but little to his muscular power. Therefore he must eat chiefly of proteids, such as meats, eggs, etc., from which he secures additional strength and proper material to replace worn-out tissue. However, if he were to continue his rigid or special diet too long, there would be a deficiency of fat and sugar, and his general health would be impaired. On the other hand, during convalescence from fevers, or where extreme emaciation exists, as in tuberculosis and various other conditions, fatty foods are urgently demanded. Aside from the temporary or special instances that have been just related, a mixed diet is regarded as essential to continue health and strength, for it contributes to the support of all tissues and functions.

It has been demonstrated that the average man requires only about 1 pound of dry food a day, which need not include more than $2\frac{1}{2}$ ounces of proteids. A man who is employed at hard muscular labor requires more food than one doing mental work. Some authorities say that the heavy meal of the day should be served after working hours, because then there is time to enjoy thoroughly what is eaten; the energies relax and give the digestive apparatus a fair chance.

One custom that has grown up with modern civilization is the necessity for regular habits in the exercise of the functions of the human body. As an instance of the regularity with which the bodily functions operate, it has been found, by comprehensive physiological tests, that at the regular meal hours the digestive juices flow more freely, digestion takes place more quickly and more surely, and both assimilation and excretion are better cared for. When regular hours of sleep can be combined with regular habits of eating, the strength of the body is conserved and promoted.

10. Fruit.—Fresh and ripe fruit, if properly used, is valuable in various ways; but as a rule dependence cannot be placed on it as an important nutritive agent; furthermore, its effect varies in each case, and the extent to which it is to be consumed must be decided by the individual.

Extremes of temperature in eating should be avoided. Food that is too hot or too cold should not be taken into the stomach. Hot foods not only blunt the sense of taste and injure the mouth, but they also weaken the stomach and digestion. Likewise, ices and ice-cold foods, especially ice water, hinder and delay digestion by lowering the stomach temperature greatly below the digestion point.

11. Exercise and Proper Food.—Exercise and proper food are the most important factors in maintaining the tone of the alimentary tract. If the laws of personal hygiene that relate to proper food and plenty of exercise are carefully obeyed, unpleasant conditions are quite sure either to disappear or to be greatly diminished. If the contrary course is followed and headache cures and cathartics are resorted to, the muscular power of the intestines as well as the general muscular system becomes still further impaired, and persons so afflicted become a prey for fakers who advertise all sorts of cures which, in the end, can prove only harmful.

12. Value of Water.—Water, next to air, is most neces-sary to life. It plays an exceedingly important part in main-taining the various functions of the body. It is constantly needed to make up for the loss of moisture from the skin and lungs, it flushes out certain organs, and also preserves the shape and symmetry of the body.

The importance of water in the preservation of health is far from being appreciated, and few persons drink enough of it. This lack of fluid may lead to unpleasant conditions, such as indigestion, torpidity, headache, dryness of the skin, etc., the cause of which is not usually understood.

It is estimated that the adult human being needs 2 or 3 quarts of water in 24 hours. Probably one-third of this is usually taken with the food. In addition, four or five glasses of water a day under ordinary conditions would be a fair estimate of what the system requires, although it is subject to great changes, depending largely on exercise and climatic con-ditions. During the warm weather, the skin rapidly abstracts large quantities of water from the system, which need to be replaced promptly. There is no objection to drinking a rea-sonable amount of water with the meals, although it should not be confined to this time, but distributed more evenly through-out the day.

The importance of water in maintaining proper health requires that the supply shall be as pure as possible. Water should not be taken into the system in too copious drafts or drunk too rapidly. The better plan is to drink one-half or one glass at a time. Early in the morning, on rising, and before retiring are two good times to drink water. Water drunk at these and at other times when the stomach is not crowded with food has a beneficial effect, and is believed by many eminent physiologists to prevent ills.

13. Care in Drinking Water.—The salesman, in traveling from one city to another, should be careful about the water he drinks. Some cities are notorious for the poor quality of the water in the city mains. Distilled water is freest from germs; boiled water is next. Water from reservoirs equipped with good sand filters is practically safe if the filters are cleaned at regular intervals. Lemon juice and lime juice have a purifying effect on water. As ice is often contaminated, water containing ordinary ice cannot be called safe; besides, authorities recommend cool water rather than water that is ice cold.

Next in value to water, as a beverage, comes the fresh unfermented juices of various fruits. In addition to satisfying the demands of thirst, they contribute food to the body without in any way taxing the digestive organs, as they are predigested by the sunshine in Nature's own laboratory.

<hr>

PROPER BATHING

14. Personal Cleanliness.—There should be no necessity to emphasize the fact that for reasons both of health and business, every man should keep himself scrupulously clean. Some men neglect bathing until their smell is offensive. Such persons usually do not realize why they are unwelcome until some one is brutally frank enough to give the reason. Others, while careful to bathe regularly, go around with black finger nails or dirty ears or teeth and prejudice many against them. Neglected teeth cause an offensive breath, which must be corrected at once, or the man will be curtly turned away, and will probably never know the reason. Offensive breath is also caused by nasal and throat affections, and by a disordered stomach.

15. Value of the Bath.—Many persons who wash their faces and hands regularly seem to think that the bathing of the entire body is something that need be done only occasionally. One of nature's methods of eliminating waste is through the pores of the skin, so that a certain amount of dead material is continually accumulating on the skin. Unless removed, this interferes with the health of the skin and consequently with the health of the body; therefore the body should be bathed daily. Friction of some kind, as with a rough wash cloth or a rubber brush, must be used to remove this waste. Persons who dislike so much bathing find a vigorous dry rub with a coarse towel very beneficial.

Contrary to popular belief, the body needs its daily cleansing as much when perspiration is not free as when it is most evident, for in the very act of perspiring some waste is carried off. But one should never bathe immediately after eating; it is better to wait several hours.

16. Cold-Water Baths.—The cold-water bath is stimulating, but should be taken in moderation. It is easy to remain in cold water too long and thus depress the forces of the body; less than 1 minute is usually ample time for this bath. The cold bath taken immediately on rising is a powerful tonic, when followed by a brisk rub so as to make the flesh glow. Those who are unaccustomed to cold-water bathing may lessen the severity by beginning with moderately cool water. Many modern hotels are equipped with shower baths; a little time under a cool shower early in the morning has a wonderfully refreshing effect and helps the salesman to start the day right. A little vigorous exercise followed by a bath of this sort will go far toward removing depression or staleness and will make the salesman feel, as one has aptly expressed it, "like a fighting cock." Comparatively few homes are fitted with shower baths; but at very small expense a very good shower arrangement over an ordinary bathtub may be provided. But the pleasure and healthfulness of bathing need not be foregone because of the lack of a bathtub. Persons who cannot stand the cold dip or cold shower find a good substitute in vigorously rubbing the entire body with a rough towel soaked in cold water.

17. Hot-Water Baths.—Hot water is of greater value as a cleanser than cold water, but a hot-water bath should always be followed by cooler water and a rub, to close the pores and excite surface circulation. The hot-water bath has a very soothing effect when taken before retiring, but a cold compress should then be applied to the head, or the effect may be stimulative instead of sedative. The hot-water bath is the proper bath when one is thoroughly chilled. Care should be taken not to remain in hot water too long, as this is apt to have a weakening effect.

_____

18. Value of Exercise.—Briefly, some of the benefits of exercise are as follows: It develops the brain, aids digestion, assimilation of food, and distribution of nourishment to the part exercised, assists the excretion of waste material through the skin and other organs of elimination, begets strength and begets symmetry. Therefore, exercise is a great factor in selling work.

Many salesmen get an abundance of that excellent form of exercise, walking, and get it in the open air; but the indoor salesman is less fortunate; his work is sometimes almost as sedentary as that of the man who works at a desk.

Many men keep in good physical condition without taking any exercise except that which they get in their regular work. A reasonable amount of special exercise is helpful, however, to one whose working conditions do not promote the all-around welfare of the body; but it is not necessary to make athletics a hobby. It is easy to build up unusual muscular development by constant practice, but the body will gradually return to normal conditions unless the muscles are used actively, and the athletes who go to extremes are not noted for their longevity.

19. Forms of Exercise.—When a gymnasium is convenient, light exercise may be taken there for promoting the efficiency of any part of the body that is neglected in the regular work, for developing a weak chest, for example. The best form of exercise, though, is that taken in a game, such as lawn tennis, golf, bowling, etc. Here, play and exercise are agreeably combined, and such exercise is an ideal form. If neither gymnasium work nor some game can be practiced, a short time spent in room exercise will prove helpful and a good preparation for the night's rest. It is not even necessary to use apparatus. Almost any movements that alternately relax and contract the muscles and promote deep breathing will prove help-

K S F—9

ful. The room should be well ventilated, and the movements should be practiced preferably when all clothing has been removed. Ordinarily 15 or 20 minutes spent in exercising will prove sufficient. It is not a good plan to become exhausted. Room exercise should always be followed by deep breathing.

REST AND RELAXATION

20. Nature demands that tired nerves be relaxed daily, and unless this demand is granted, destructive results are bound to follow. So every man owes it to himself, to his physical and mental health, to leave his work entirely alone at least once daily and give both the body and the mind a rest. Some men keep their work on their minds at night as heavily as during the day, even dreaming about it. The enthusiast, the concentrator, can hardly dismiss his business from his mind entirely when he gets home, nor is it necessary, for often the best business ideas come in moments of relaxation. But the strain should be thrown off and the mind diverted to other things for a while. A good social talk, a pleasant evening of entertainment, any relaxing diversion, gives rest and new points of view. Something of a very annoying nature that happened during the day and that preyed on the mind will recede to its proper place and be thought of more calmly the next day. Some men make it a rule never to reply to a harsh or impertinent letter on the day it is received, but to wait until the next day, after the relaxation of the evening has enabled them to deal calmly and judiciously with the matter.

An important practical point is for each man to ascertain the signs of fatigue, so that he may know how best to act. When sleep is constantly disturbed with dreams about one's work and the dreamer becomes restless, fatigue may be the predominant cause. When one is indisposed to work, is tired of it, the cause may be fatigue—or it may be laziness. Bearing this in mind, under normal conditions it is not difficult to discover the real cause; but the trouble is, when a man is fatigued, his judgment seems affected, and he is apt to ascribe his lack of vigor to some other origin. The best general way for sizing one's self up in this respect is to look at one's daily life as an outsider, and to ask this question: If this person I am looking at were some other person, with just the same make-up, and were living just the way in which I am living, would that person be fatigued? This logical device is often a great help in determining whether one needs a resolution or a rest.

Sundays, holidays, and vacations must all be taken into consideration. They are for rest and refreshment; they should end by finding a man more sure of himself than he was before.

The needs and habits of men vary so that it is difficult to lay down definite rules about the amount of sleep that should be taken. The average man requires 8 hours of sound sleep to keep at his best; some exceptional men get along with 6 hours. One who sleeps more than 10 hours overdoes it. Every one should cultivate the habit of leaving cares behind when retiring. A good bath and deep-breathing exercises are the best aids toward a perfect night's rest; sleep-producing drugs are dangerous and should be avoided. Sleep is the body's great recuperator and a great blessing. It should be treasured. He who plays fast and loose with his sleeping hours will sooner or later pay the penalty.

***

KEEPING WELL IN WARM WEATHER

21. Food and Drinks.—Cold weather is rather stimulating and acts as a tonic to the system; but warm weather is enervating and relaxing, and is apt to cause depression and other uncomfortable feelings to persons in poor physical condition. Furthermore, warm weather is very destructive to foodstuffs and other products, as decomposition rapidly ensues, for germs or bacteria multiply much faster when the temperature is high.

The discomfort of hot weather may be greatly relieved by a careful selection of food and drink, in order to diminish the work thrown upon the stomach and intestines; for during this period of the year these organs are apt to be less well prepared to perform their functions than at other times, and the food is not always fresh and good. Meat, particularly when it is taken in large quantities, undergoes fermentation and putrefaction in the intestinal tract, which is largely the cause of the discomfort that often follows its use, and is much more marked during the warm weather. Therefore, meat should be sparingly eaten during the summer.

Fish is a good summer food; but it must be obtained fresh, for it decomposes very rapidly in warm weather, and if eaten in this condition may cause unpleasant and even serious results.

Cereals, fresh vegetables, and fruit are also very valuable articles of diet during warm weather.

22. Relaxation in Summer.—A vacation is a very important aid in preserving good physical condition during the summer; but a large part of the population of a city cannot enjoy this pleasure and must depend on some form of night or day entertainment and relaxation. Unfortunately, most people in the United States do not select the recreation that is of most value to them. They are far behind European countries, where the most suitable and valuable means of rest and comfort are secured at the minimum cost.

A quiet inland place should be selected for a day's outing. While sea air has its advantages, but little benefit is derived from it in a day's excursion, particularly when the weather is hot and there is a constant exposure to the direct rays of the sun. Many inland places provide shade, quiet, a lower temperature, and an abundant supply of good drinking water, the latter being a very important consideration. A luncheon taken from home offers far more pleasure than the purchase of food of a questionable character. These conditions offer a better opportunity for rest and recuperation.

The summer months possess the normal climatic conditions of a certain season of the year and people will not suffer unduly if they are properly prepared for it. In other words, they must, so far as possible, keep themselves in good physical condition at all times, the question of diet, etc., being a part of personal hygiene.

Hot and cold weather, like disease, select for their victims those who are in poor health or who are careless about their physical condition, while, on the other hand, those who present a formidable resisting power are but little affected by the various climatic changes.

23. Protection Against Cold Weather.—Upon the approach of winter, the custom, at least in the United States, is to make certain changes both in under and outer garments. While the various details usually carried out in this direction may appear reasonable and logical, they are not altogether in harmony with modern sanitation.

In protecting against cold weather, two factors are to be dealt with; care of the body, and proper selection of clothing. A previous article has stated the importance of exercise and proper food, and also the value of the cold sponge or shower bath judiciously employed to secure a healthy condition of the body, thus providing a very formidable resisting power against the unpleasant conditions that may follow changes in temperature. The protection afforded by these hygienic measures is more valuable in winter than in summer, for they render important aid in retaining the body heat, and those who pay careful attention to this matter, particularly in early life, are as a rule able to stand very marked changes in weather with little or no discomfort. Except possibly in the extreme northern part of the United States, medium-weight woolen underclothing is usually sufficient for all purposes, the heavy weight being reserved rather for long outside exposure, particularly when a person is not exercising.

24. Treatment of Colds.—The germs that cause a cold may at almost any time be found in the nose and throat. The exciting cause which will render them sufficiently active to induce inflammation may come in the form of lowered vitality, or drafts, wet feet, sudden changes of temperature, etc. People in the mountains or in regions where there is little chance of infection do not suffer from colds, although the temperature may be very low and the exposure long.

As a cold is a germ infection, it must follow a certain course and the best that can be done, under the circumstances, is to lessen its severity and prevent its extension. A popular belief, in which there is considerable truth, is that a cold lasts three days. Even when properly cared for, the activity of the attack seldom ceases in less time.

A cold is ushered in by symptoms so well known that they need hardly be described. In a well-marked case a feeling of depression usually precedes the more active symptoms, such as chilliness, sneezing, and dryness of the membrane of the nostrils, followed by a copious discharge, pains in different parts of the body, sometimes accompanied by considerable elevation of temperature. If the attack is associated with the constitutional symptoms referred to, much time will be saved and many unpleasant complications avoided if the patient will remain at home and in a room which is kept at an even temperature of about 70° until the more active symptoms have subsided. There is also less chance of transmitting the infection to others—particularly where cleanliness is observed and the discharges are promptly destroyed. Thin sterilized cheesecloth, cut in small pieces, should be used in place of handkerchiefs and afterwards burned.

If the symptoms are aggravated, the family physician should be promptly sent for; otherwise, some of the simple home remedies may be employed. In the beginning a hot lemonade, extra warmth to the body, and a cathartic at bedtime are of value; for these agents stimulate the skin, liver, and intestinal tract and aid in relieving the inflamed membrane and limiting the infection. A mustard foot bath at bedtime may also be useful. The diet should be light and without meat.

Far more important in connection with this subject are preventive measures. These may be practically applied by observing the rules of hygiene, good food, proper exercise, cold baths, etc., for all of these protect against colds by keeping the body in a healthy condition.

Proper clothing should be worn, suitable for the season. Such articles as chest protectors and mufflers should be avoided, for they weaken the skin and therefore do more harm than good. The care of the body, rather than the selection of the clothing, offers the greatest protection in the prevention of colds.

Wet feet constitute one of the most common causes of a cold, particularly as the stockings and shoes usually remain wet or damp for the greater part of the day. The unpopularity of rubbers, because of their appearance, is unreasonable, in view of the great comfort and protection afforded by them in wet weather. Rain coats are also of great value in keeping the clothing dry during storms, for umbrellas at the best protect only the head and upper part of the body. If wet clothing, shoes, and stockings cannot be promptly changed, a cold may often be prevented if active exercise is continued until an opportunity presents itself to rub the skin briskly and put on dry garments.

A person who has contracted a very mild cold can hardly be expected to remain at home, particularly if it interferes with the daily work; but effort should be made to prevent further infection by avoiding undue exposure while in this condition, otherwise a mild attack often becomes a severe one and may last indefinitely or end in some unpleasant or serious complication.

USE OF STIMULANTS

25. Introduction.—The consideration of stimulants and their use opens up some interesting situations, for notwithstanding the fact that the weight of scientific evidence is decidedly against stimulants as an asset in personal efficiency, it is a fact that the use of stimulants is widespread.

Ranging all the way from such beverages as tea and coffee to the use of opiates, the entire human race seems to be prone to the use of stimulants.

The salesman, however, who wants to become efficient, should not permit himself to fall into the error of thinking he can either increase his physical strength and endurance or brighten his mentality through the use of artificial stimulants, for, as has been emphasized in previous paragraphs, pure air, food, water, and proper exercises are the fundamentals of both physical and mental and, indeed, we should add moral, strength.

The most common stimulants used by the people of this country are alcoholic liquors and tobacco. The effect of each is so universally known that it is unnecessary for us to enter into a lengthy discussion of these things, but the following points should be noted.

26. Alcohol.—There is overwhelming argument from the moral and scientific points of view against the use of strong drink. While some men drink moderately with apparent impunity, those who develop the habit take a risk. Without entering into the moral side of the drink question, it may be put down as a plain business principle that the salesman who takes a drink before he calls on a prospect, or on a man who may possibly disapprove of the use of intoxicants, is taking chances. Many persons absolutely decline to do business with men who have been using intoxicants; therefore, it is clearly to a salesman's interests to be temperate at all times, and to drink nothing where it may possibly injure his business. The salesman, going from hotel to hotel and often feeling lonely, has unusual temptation to drink, and the habit thus formed has been the ruin of many thousands of brilliant salesmen. The number of employers who refuse to engage men who use intoxicants is constantly increasing, and the form of salesmanship that included getting drunk with the prospect before attempting to do business with him is obsolete. The "man of the hour" in salesmanship is the man who wins on clean lines—not on his conviviality.

27. Tobacco.—While little or nothing can be said in favor of the use of tobacco, it is unnecessary to do more than caution against excessive use and to remind a salesman that it is often decidedly objectionable to the other man to have a salesman smoke during the interview. Many men do not smoke and are considerably annoyed by the fumes of tobacco. A salesman should throw away a cigar before walking into an office, unless he is certain that smoking will not be objectionable.

APPEARANCE

IMPORTANCE OF APPROPRIATE DRESS

28. Effect on the Wearer.—Notwithstanding the oft repeated axiom, "Dress does not make the man," and the universally emphasized thought that, as men learn each other thoroughly, they think more of the solid qualities of character and less of clothes, correct speech, etc., the stern and unchangeable fact remains that in business life a man's success often depends largely on the early impressions that he makes. The first impression has such a bearing on sales work that a man runs a risk if he presents himself in any but the most favorable manner.

Appropriate dress has two distinct effects: The effect on the wearer himself and the effect on those with whom he comes in contact. Success in selling goods, or success in molding opinions in any other direction, depends largely on a man's poise, his sureness of himself, and his satisfaction with himself. A man may be possessed of excellent qualities, that would ordinarily win; but let him feel that he is not at his best, and his force is greatly lessened.

A man knows when he presents the correct appearance, and he is greatly buoyed up by the consciousness that he looks his best. A man cannot appear in a shabby coat or a dirty collar before a well-dressed audience and do justice to himself. Thousands of discouraged men could be helped to get on their feet again by being well washed, well fed, and well dressed. A bath, a shave, clean linen, and a new suit will often work wonders.

There is no excuse for a man's going around habitually in baggy, spotted clothes, when in most towns a suit can be pressed for a half dollar and cleaned for a little more. The salesman who wears a soiled collar, whose suit looks as if he slept in it, and whose shoes look as if he had just come out of a lumber camp, has a great handicap to overcome.

It may be argued that the man who is conscious of being

K S F—10

well dressed is likely to display his consciousness; such consciousness, however, is shown only temporarily. A man accustomed to wearing slouchy clothes may actually feel and appear awkward when he changes his style of dress for the better; he may show the change as plainly as the youngster shows his consciousness of his "Sunday clothes." But when once the habit of dressing properly becomes fixed, a man should be able to follow Lord Chesterfield's famous advice to be scrupulously careful of his dress and then think no more about it. In fact, one distinguishing feature of a well-dressed man is the quiet unassuming manner with which he wears his clothes. Therefore, the first thing gained by being well dressed is the wearer's feeling that he looks the part he is expected to play. He has started out by building up self-respect, and when he respects himself he can reasonably hope to command respect from others.

29. Effect on the Prospect.—It is idle to say that it is the inner man that counts, so long as men form their judgments by what they see. The eye takes in the outer man at a glance, while it may be months before the character is understood and appreciated. In some kinds of selling work, personal appearance may be of minor importance. For instance, the man going through rural districts selling fruit trees need not be dressed as carefully as the investment or encyclopedia salesman. But salesmen ordinarily are expected to be clean, well-appearing men, and the man who goes before a prospect otherwise is taking the chances of making a poor impression. The prospect will probably say nothing about the ill-fitting or shabby coat, the baggy trousers, the loud necktie, or the conspicuous shoes of the salesman; but his impression will be unfavorable and the salesman may be dismissed with one of the common excuses that prospects give. When it is considered what a critical time the moment of approach is, it would seem that any salesman would have the good sense to have everything possible in his favor; yet scores of salesmen are daily turned away with scant consideration because their appearance or manners were against them.

The well-dressed man may be actually inferior mentally to some salesman who is careless of his appearance, yet because the well-appearing man is careful of his dress and evidently respects himself, he commands the favorable consideration of those he meets. Men expect to find something distinctive in the salesman who shows good judgment and taste in the selection of his clothing. He appears at the outset, at least, to be above the average. While the well-dressed man may have no more, or even considerably less, money than the poorly dressed man, the fact that he is dressed in good taste is an indication that he is successful, and success commands respect and attention. Hence the money invested in appropriate dress that will increase materially the salesman's chance of securing favorable consideration is his most profitable investment.

DETAILS OF APPROPRIATE DRESS

SUITS

30. Price of Clothing.—To men who have been accustomed to buying moderate-priced clothing, the payment of $50, $60, $70, or even more for a suit appears to be the height of extravagance; and yet a high-priced suit, if bought with good judgment, will often wear as long as two cheap suits and be better looking all the time. But no practical rule can be laid down as to the price that salesmen should pay for their clothes. Some salesmen's work is not of the character that requires the best clothing. Thousands of salesmen, particularly young men just entering the field, feel they cannot afford to pay more than a moderate price for a suit of clothes. But where so much depends on good appearance, it is better to be a little better dressed than is necessary than to fall below a fair standard. No one should go into debt for the sake of making a good appearance; every man of good sense should so lay out his money as to keep within his means and be free from the annoyance of debts that he cannot meet. The amount of the expenditure should be regulated according to the salesman's earning ability and the character of his work.

The man whose expenditure for clothing must be small should watch opportunities for getting good value for his money. By keeping in touch with the leading men's clothing stores and the moderate-priced tailoring shops in the dull seasons, he will be able to obtain good bargains. Some men make it a rule to buy late in the season when merchants lower their prices in order to close out the season's supply. As men's styles do not change radically, this plan usually works well, particularly if a conservative style of clothing is selected. The man who can afford the higher-priced clothes should patronize a reliable tailor as long as he gives first-class service. The tailor who spends his entire time in making clothes and in studying fabrics and styles is in a position to give valuable advice as to what will wear well, what becomes the wearer, etc. Time should be taken to select something that will give lasting satisfaction.

31. Style of Clothes.—Of course, styles in men's clothing change from season to season, and a definite rule specifying detail of correct dress for particular occasions one season, might be out of place within a very short time. And, therefore, a man of good business sense always guards against extremes. The extremist in dress cannot properly be called the well-dressed man. Much, of course, must be left to individual taste. Some men, with the idea of being conservative, dress in a style that is hardly adapted to the forceful business man. More salesmen probably err in too conspicuous dressing than in over-conservatism. The salesman's work is one that will ordinarily stand clothing of fairly distinct types, but the goods he sells have a bearing on this question. The dress that would be appropriate for a man on the road selling sporting goods might be decidedly inappropriate for a salesman in the famous jewelry store of Tiffany & Co.

32. Relation of Height and Weight to Style of Suit.—A coat that is cut right for a man 5 feet 11 inches tall who weighs 175 pounds is not necessarily suitable for a man of slightly different height and weight. The good tailor will always have keen regard for not only height and weight, but for even such details as the size of shoe that a man wears. The well-dressed man will be careful that his coat is not so short as to give him the appearance of an overgrown boy, even if the style tendency does run to short coats.

A rule that works well is that the coat of the business suit should come down to the point reached by one's fingers when standing at ease with the arm at the side and the hand opened. This rule fails only when one has extremely long or short arms, and then the person knows it, and can tell about what would be the normal length. In connection with the length of the coat, becomingness should be considered before fashion. However popular any color, cut, or cloth may be, if it is not becoming, the individual who wears it is not well dressed, for becomingness is the fundamental law of correct dress.

33. Number of Suits.—It is economy to have two business suits, that can be worn alternately. To wear a different suit at the beginning of each week is an agreeable change, and each suit wears better by having a rest and a little attention. In many cities there are shops that, for a small sum, will send for a suit, clean, press, and deliver it every week. This arrangement is very convenient for the salesman who is much at home; but the man who travels much must adopt some other plan. All modern hotels now have facilities for pressing clothes overnight either on the premises or near by.

34. Selection of Fabrics.—In selecting a suit, attention should be paid to both the wearing quality of the goods and the appropriateness of the color to the man who is to wear the suit. A piece of goods that is very loosely woven is not likely to wear particularly well, while a fabric that has too hard a twist is likely to become shiny soon. In this matter, the man who is not expert in judging fabrics should rely on the judgment of a conscientious tailor or clothing salesman. Unless the salesman is in an extreme climate, he should select neither very light nor very heavy weights; the season in which the moderately light or moderately heavy goods may be worn is longer, and new clothing need not be purchased so often. The use of underwear of different weights is better than attempting to have suits of so many different weights. For business use, a suit should be of such color that it will stand service without fading or showing spots. Very dark solid or nearly solid colors do not meet these requirements as well as medium colors or goods that have a decided mixture.

The most serviceable fabrics for general wear are the rough-finished goods, those having a nap or fuzzy surface, and the best among these are cheviots. They wear longest because when the nap has disappeared there is still a hard finish that will show gloss less quickly than a cloth that was originally *finished,* or hard.

35. Selection of Colors.—In the choice of colors, it is well to remember that white intensifies any color, while black has the opposite effect. So the lighter the suit, the more pronounced becomes a man's coloring, while the darker the suit, the less noticeable is any physical characteristic, such as a florid face or red hair. Likewise the lighter the object, the larger it appears to the observer. A large, stout man in a light suit looks stouter, while his size appears reduced in a dark suit. Similarly, a slim man looks still more slender in dark clothes; he should wear a light suit because it will make him look broader than he really is.

Plaids and checks make one look larger and broader, and stripes increase the height. A stout man, therefore, should avoid light colors, as well as plaids and checks; he should wear dark fabrics and stripes. The slim man should avoid dark colors and stripes and should wear light clothes in plaids, checks, and the more pronounced mixtures.

Conspicuous colors or patterns in suits should be avoided for several reasons. The wearer tires of such suits quickly, and people who see him frequently, having his garments forced upon their attention, soon get the impression that he wears the same suit almost constantly, though he may be wearing two or three suits. Only a man who can have several business suits in wearable condition at a time, can select the louder patterns. Even then, the more pronounced the color or pattern, the greater is the danger of bad taste in the selection, and the greater the necessity for extreme care to avoid discord in the choice of the accessories. With a chocolate shade of brown, for instance, one must give especial attention to the selection of his tie and shirt or he will get a combination of colors that will create an unfavorable impression, subconsciously perhaps, on every one he meets. On the other hand, any color harmonizes with gray, because gray is neutral. Green is trying to men and should not be worn by a man who spends moderately on clothing. Blue always looks neat, though if it is a decided blue the wearer will have the same difficulty as to color harmony as with brown. If one has a gray suit with little or no color in it, his second suit may well be blue or brown mixed with gray so as to relieve the basic color.

_____

OVERCOATS

36. The overcoat is a garment that may be worn the greater part of the year, but, of course, the proper weight depends upon the season. In the early fall and late spring, a very light weight top coat is always in good taste. Later in the fall, a coat of heavier material is always not only comfortable throughout the greater portion of this country, but is at the same time correct so far as style is concerned. Then, in extremely cold or stormy weather, one should have a heavy overcoat. By keeping three, or at least two coats of different weights, you can make your overcoats last a long time.

The general styles of overcoats change from year to year just as styles of other wearing apparel change. Some years fur collars or plush collars or collars of the same material as the rest of the garment, are in vogue and, of course, the man who wishes to be properly dressed—as the salesman always should be—and must wear an overcoat two or more seasons should be careful to select styles that are conservative and not likely to change greatly.

The man who does not wish to buy a new overcoat every year, should avoid extremes, such as odd pockets, cuffs, buttons, etc., for these things are always comparatively short-lived and do not remain in style as long as the average overcoat should wear.

The overcoat should always be darker than the suit with which it is worn, for pleasing effect. A man who buys but one overcoat in a year should have it of medium weight and preferably of a dark-gray mixture, which is known as the Oxford gray. A man who buys two overcoats in a year should have one for general wear of the style described and one of plain, or almost plain, black for evening and Sunday wear.

HATS

37. As with a suit, a hat should be selected with proper consideration of the height, weight, and coloring of the wearer. A black hat can, of course, be worn well by almost any type of man. A man can easily get a hat that is too high or that has too broad a brim for his face; or he may make the other mistake and get a small hat, which will give him the appearance of an overgrown boy wearing his last year's hat.

Becomingness is the first consideration in choosing the hat. Neither good taste, good form, nor sound judgment are shown in wearing a hat that is unsuited to one's head. Well-dressed men usually find a style of hat that looks well on them and stick to it, despite changes in popular fancy.

SHIRTS

38. There is so much room for individual taste in the selecting of shirts that only a few general suggestions need be given. The caution to buy no shirts of loud colors is, however, in order. Stripes of a fairly strong color do not necessarily make a shirt loud, if the stripe is fine and inconspicuous. But pinks, greens, etc., are likely to be in poor taste unless the maker has handled the color well.

NECKWEAR

39. It has been truly said that no article of dress reflects a man's good taste or his poor taste more quickly than his necktie. Cheap purchases are generally unsatisfactory, but a cheap necktie seems to advertise its cheapness more quickly than any other article of a man's attire. It pays to buy first-class neck-wear and to discard a tie as soon as it becomes soiled or wrinkled beyond repair. A good tie will stand several times as much wear without wrinkling as a poor one, since the makers choose not only the best colors but the best-tying material for the higher-priced goods.

The wearer must take account of the color of the shirt and suit to be worn before deciding on the color of the tie. For example, a shirt of decided blue seldom harmonizes well with a green tie; only an expert colorist can match blue and green harmoniously. A tie of dark red or reddish brown will go well with a tan shirt.

Very light colors in neckties are more appropriate for light suits than for dark suits. An excellent feature of the gray mixtures in suits is that they permit a wide range in ties; well-selected greens, reds, blues, and browns may be worn with good taste. There are so many tints, shades, and hues of colors that it is not enough to say that certain colors go well together. Some greens, blues, and reds, for example, make handsome ties; others are too strong for general wear. One who is not a prac-tical colorist should ask the advice of close friends occasionally as to color combinations. Women are often excellent critics of personal appearance, appropriate colors, etc. The salesman, by consulting others, may find that he is unconsciously showing himself to be a man of poor taste. By seeing himself as others see him, the faults may be corrected.

SHOES

40. The man who must be on his feet much needs com-fort and a good thick sole to his shoes. Whatever one may think of buying high-priced suits, he can certainly have no doubt, after wearing a few pairs of high-grade shoes, of the greater satisfaction and economy to be secured by buying shoes of superior grade. Shoes, like suits, give better service when not worn continuously. When a shoe is taken off, a shoe tree should be put into it, so that it will not lose shape as the warmth and moisture drawn from the body leave the leather. It seems hardly necessary to lay emphasis on getting a good fit; but men frequently buy shoes that fit imperfectly, with the result that the shoes are either uncomfortable or lose shape quickly.

There is nothing in moderately priced shoes that surpasses good calfskin; but unless it has a special finish, such as the gun-metal finish, calfskin, particularly when first bought, requires more frequent polishing than leathers of more shiny finish and hence the shoes are not always convenient for the salesman. It is well to remember that a foot looks larger in a tan than in a black shoe.

The caution to avoid extremes applies as well to shoes as to other articles of dress; the careful dresser never aims to make himself an advertiser of fancy tops or other novel effects.

MISCELLANEOUS POINTS ABOUT APPEARANCE

41. Accessories of Dress.—Hard-and-fast rules concerning the things men of particular coloring should wear are difficult to mention, because some men go contrary to accepted standards and still dress in fairly good taste. Some men can carry more than others. However, generally speaking, the man of light coloring should wear modest effects. Only a dark-haired or swarthy man can stand vivid hues. It should be remembered that not only the color of the suit, but also the color of the necktie and shirt must be considered, because the latter are in closer proximity to the face.

To a man of unusual physical proportions, also, the selection of the accessories in juxtaposition to his face becomes a matter of prime importance. These are the hat, collar, tie, and shirt. A man with a long thin face should give preference to cross effects and a man of full face should choose up-and-down effects. Thus, a man of long, thin face should wear a hat with a flattish set brim and a moderate crown, a wing instead of a fold collar, a bow tie instead of a four-in-hand, and a shirt with plaid or figured pattern. A full-faced man should select a hat with well-curled brim, a fold collar, a four-in-hand tie, and a shirt with vertical stripes.

42. Clean Linen.—A salesman should have enough collars to be able to wear a spotless one at all times. In some cities it is advisable to change even oftener than once a day. It is no economy to continue wearing frayed or soiled linen. The eyes of the prospect seem to fall on little details more quickly than on other things; in fact, human judgment seems to be based very often on trifles.

43. Good Carriage.—Many men do not carry themselves well and thus fail to make the best appearance. It would be an excellent thing if every man had enough military experience to develop the habit of standing and walking well; but as this is impracticable, the habit should be formed of holding the head and shoulders up and looking the world squarely in the face. The habit of slouching along with the body bent over or of sprawling out when a seat is taken is one of those small things that may occasionally keep a man from making the best impression. One's carriage really has some relation to his mental attitude, as may be plainly seen by comparing the attitudes of the discouraged man and the optimistic, aggressive man. Therefore, to stimulate his mental powers, a man should carry himself erect and fearlessly, as if he found the world a good place to live in, and looked forward with pleasure to meeting his fellow men.

MEMORY HELPS

He who can answer the following questions from memory has a good understanding of the text in the preceding pages.

(1) Name six factors of good health.

(2) Why is pure air of vital importance?

(3) Describe the proper method of breathing.

(4) What is a common fault with respect to the quantity of food eaten?

(5) Why is it essential to chew food thoroughly?

(6) Why is it inadvisable to drink a great deal while eating?

(7) What are the objections to extremely hot and cold foods?

(8) Why is it vitally important for the salesman to keep himself scrupulously clean?

(9) Compare the advantages of hot- and of cold-water baths.

(10) What benefits are derived from a good form of exercise?

(11) What are the approved ideas in regard to rest and relaxation?

(12) In selecting suits what points should be taken into consideration?

(13) What should be one's guide in the selection of neckties?

(14) What are the arguments against conspicuous clothes?

(15) What is the value of erect carriage to the salesman?

CPSIA information can be obtained at www.ICGtesting.com
Printed in the USA
BVOW01s2237140813

328731BV00013B/265/P